WOODLAND

POND

POOL HOUSE

AVIARY

VEGETABLES

An Affair with a House

AN AFFAIR
WITH A HOUSE

BUNNY WILLIAMS

WITH CHRISTINE PITTEL

PHOTOGRAPHS BY FRITZ VON DER SCHULENBERG, RICHARD FELBER, ERIC STRIFFLER,
JOE STANDART, AND JENNIFER GREENBERG.
BOOK DESIGN BY DOUG TURSHEN, WITH DAVID HUANG

Stewart, Tabori & Chang, New York

ACKNOWLEDGMENTS

I never would have thought to do this book without the vision and encouragement of my friend Fritz von der Schulenburg. He planted the idea in my head, and when I saw his beautiful photographs of my home, I found the courage to tackle this project. It is to him I owe the creation of this book.

To Doug Turshen, who took all the components and made magic on the page. Collaborating with him was a pleasure.

To Richard Felber, who always makes the garden look better than it is. To Joe Standart, who took the beautiful pictures of Alan's house, and to Eric Striffler, who captured the joys of entertaining.

To Christine Pittel, who distilled all the scribbles and conversations into a text the reader can enjoy.

To Sandy Gilbert, who was a great conductor and made all the parts come together for the grand finale. And to Christina Juarez, who made sure this book was going to happen and helped keep me on track.

To the memory of my parents, from whom my love of houses, gardens, dogs, and entertaining all grew.

And especially to my husband John Rosselli, who really made all of my dreams come true.

TABLE OF CONTENTS

INTRODUCTION

I am not sure if I believe in destiny, but I do know that after years of looking for a house, my palms began to perspire when I turned onto a tree-lined driveway in a small New England village. As I approached the white clapboard house hidden under towering old locusts and maples, I felt that I was meant to be here and fell in love with the place—peeling paint, unkempt lawn, overgrown shrubs and all. Without even going inside, I somehow knew I was home.

I got out of the car and began a tour around the building. At the back, a two-story lattice porch reminded me of the plantation homes in Virginia where I grew up. I was sure someone from the South had lived here at one time. Later, I came to learn that the main part of Manor House was built in 1840 by a man named Daniel Brewster as a home for his Southern bride. The classic Federal house, with an unusual semi-elliptical window glazed in a globe pattern on the front pediment, was attached to a small 18th-century homestead that belonged to the Brewster family. Originally, the lattice porch wrapped three sides of the house, presumably to make his wife feel more at home. Only the back portion remains. The side porch, at some point, was remodeled and screened-in. The long L-shaped wing, now converted to a series of service rooms, was once a single-story carriage shed. In the 1930s, the roof was raised and a series of dormer windows were added to extend the house.

By the time I arrived, the property had been broken up and all that was left of the larger farm was twelve acres and a wonderful 1840 barn that was used as the garage. The grounds were in terrible condition and any gardens were long gone, but there was an amazing collection of mature trees, including calupas, locust, apple, white birch, and various types of large pine and hemlock. As I walked around, all I could think of were the flowerbeds and borders I could not wait to plant. Immediately I envisioned a sunken garden on the south side of the house in a flat, grassy area bordered by lilac hedges. All it needed was a stone wall.

OPPOSITE: *There is always room on our laps for the dogs. Here John and I are joined by Charlie, an adopted mutt, Brewster, a Norfolk terrier, and Elizabeth, a very beautiful—and very spoiled—whippet.*

Across the road was a beautiful Greek Revival house that had been built by Mr. Brewster for his son. Instantly, I thought that this would be a great home for my dear friend Alan Campbell, but that is another story, for later.

Having come full circle, I found myself back at the front door of Manor House. With the excitement of a child going to the circus, I opened it. I peered into the side hall, where a simple curved staircase rose to the second floor. The walls were covered in a drab 19th-century wallpaper simulating gray stone blocks. Off to the left was the front parlor, with a mattress on the floor and clothes strewn about (the place was being used as a rooming house). But I looked beyond the mess to the four French doors with sunlight streaming in and was happy to see that the original mantel was still intact. I could imagine a fire blazing and big, comfortable armchairs. Next was a long room furnished like a college fraternity, which I immediately thought could be a library with bookcases at each end. It led to the dining room, which had a naked light bulb dangling from the ceiling. Three of the walls were covered with three different wallpapers—the fourth was left inexplicably bare. At a card table in the center, four people were playing bridge. In my mind's eye, I replaced it with a round table, set with beautiful china and candles, in this perfectly square room (I've always loved square dining rooms). Next was the kitchen—what a wreck! Vintage 1930s, with no counter space. Doors and windows everywhere, but it too had a wonderful fireplace. This would really take some planning—a complete re-do. I headed upstairs and stepped into each bedroom, dodging more clothes. Yet through the dirt and disorder I could see a glorious house that just needed love and care.

And so I came to live at Manor House and began the long and happy process of making the house into a home. There have been many changes in my life over the 30 years since I first walked through that front door. I opened my own decorating business. My first marriage dissolved. But no matter what was going on, my attachment to the house never wavered. It was my refuge. I was always happy to be here.

I'm not the type to do up a house and move on. I bought this with the thought that I could live here forever, and Manor House has grown along with me. I'll fix one thing one year, another the next. The design has evolved over a long period of time, which I think makes it even richer. I feel the same way about gardens. Once you plant a tree, you want to stick around to see what it's going to look like in 20 years.

That's why it's so fortunate that I fell in love with John Rosselli. He feels exactly the same way about houses and gardens. I remember the first time he came to Manor House. We had just driven back from a 10-day shopping spree in Maine (in 110° weather) for our yet-to-be-opened garden shop, Treillage, and we were exhilarated and exhausted. Brewster, my beloved Norfolk terrier, took to John immediately (a very good sign since he basically liked nobody but me) and John immediately took to the kitchen. We needed some nourishment, and he's an inspired cook. I was nervous about having him here. He has extraordinary taste, and I knew I couldn't possibly have enough of his beloved blue-and-white china to impress him. But John noticed things I had bought from his Manhattan antiques shop and was delighted to see them again.

He loved Manor House, and his encouragement and his eye have helped make it even more special. It was John's idea to convert the barn into one great big glorious room for entertaining. Thanks to him, chickens arrived on the property. The vegetable garden was expanded to suit his culinary needs. By the time I come down to breakfast in the morning, he's already been out feeding the chicks and searching through the vines to find the ripest tomatoes. It's a great bond when the person who shares your life also shares your passion for a place. Now it's not just my house, it's our house.

Up in the attic, I found a trunk labeled Manor House, with some musty old World War I army uniforms inside. There's a stenciled design on the floorboards up there, symbols of some sort that may date from the time this was a safe house for runaway slaves, or at least that's the rumor. The house comes with stories. I like to think they're true

MANOR HOUSE

MANOR HOUSE

It was the grandest house in town, with living room, library, dining room, kitchen, laundry, and six bedrooms—five with their own baths, a true luxury for an old house. But Manor House had been on the market for years, the white elephant of this quiet Connecticut village. Clearly not too many people were eager to take it on. After the contract was signed, I asked my father to come up and have a look. We walked all around the house together, and he didn't say a word. Finally, he turned to me and announced, "It's a wonderful house, and I'm very glad you're young."

Any rational being would have considered all the work that needed to be done and walked away. But buying a house is like falling in love—you don't see the bad parts. Immediately, my first husband and I decided that any of the work we could possibly do, we would do ourselves. So for the next seven months, we spent every weekend from 9:00 in the morning until 9:00 at night scraping paint, stripping off wallpaper, and repainting. It was always a work in progress. The mantel in the kitchen must have been covered with 50 coats of paint. I scraped off layer after layer until I got down to the raw pine.

We had to put on a new roof right away, because it was leaking, and remodel the antiquated kitchen. Other than that, most of what we did was cosmetic. Luckily, the rooms were intact, the moldings still there. All the improvements that had been made to the house in the 1930s were nicely done—simple white tile bathrooms with white porcelain pedestal sinks. I could clean them and move on.

At first, I focused on only a few rooms—the kitchen to cook in, the bedroom to sleep in, and the library to sit in. I didn't care about the living room. It sat empty for four years. I painted it off-white and put a garden bench in there, which meant there was plenty of room for the tree every Christmas.

I understood that decorating is a process that takes time. I had big plans—I was going to bring this house back to life.

OPPOSITE: *Charlie and Lucy, both adopted from the pound, race down the old brick path leading to the front door. The walkway is lined with boxwood balls, grown from tiny shrubs I planted 20 years ago.*

The porch off the dining room is home to a very special 19th-century Russian garden bench, made of wood with elaborate cast-iron arms. The original paint color has faded to a soft green. OPPOSITE: There's something so pure about the way the white clapboard house meets the green lawn, and I didn't want to mask it with plantings around the foundation.

ABOVE: *When I couldn't even get grass to grow under the shade of an old, enormous maple tree by the back door, I made this flagstone terrace and enclosed it with an elegant white picket fence.* OPPOSITE: *The cast stone table, resembling tree trunks twined with leaves, was made in France. I like the shape of the old rusty chimney pot, which would have sat on a chimney to deflect the rain and improve the draft.*

THE LIVING ROOM

I was inspired to turn my attention to the living room after a visit to the Villa San Michele in Italy, where I had taken some friends for the most expensive lunch I've ever had in my life. We sat on a loggia overlooking Florence and the cypress-covered hills of Fiesole, and the sun warmed the villa's old plaster walls. They were the most beautiful color—it was like being inside a ripe peach. I decided that this was the color I wanted for my living room and thought, how am I going to remember it? The table linens had been dyed the exact same shade and, after signing the American Express bill, I thought I'd just slip one of the napkins into my pocketbook. But with the waiter staring, I couldn't risk it. When I got back to Manor House, recreating that color became a little project.

I didn't want a refined paint job. I wanted the look of old plaster. Milk paint would give me that flat, chalky finish, but I didn't have any on hand. All oil-based paint has a sheen, so that left latex. Luckily I learned how to mix colors in art school, so I just sat down with the paint and tried to reconstruct the color from memory. I mixed white and red and yellow—with a little umber to tone it down. I worked in coffee cups, and then I would paint a patch on white cardboard to test it out.

Latex dries very quickly so you can see the color within a short period of time. I just kept going with cup after cup until I got it. But color was only half the problem. I also had to get the right texture. I thinned it down with water because I was after a slightly transparent effect. I put the paint on with a wide brush instead of a roller so you could see the brushstrokes right through it—more like a wash than a thick coat. I managed to make one section between the doors look good, but then I ran out of paint. That's the problem with working in coffee cups. Suddenly you have to figure out what the formula would be for several gallons.

Heading to the hardware store with my cardboard sample was not the answer. I think the whole idea that computers can mix paint is overrated. When it's done by machine, the colors

OPPOSITE: *The walls in the entrance hall are painted the loveliest shade of melon. I stenciled the old pine floorboards to add a little definition to the space. A stately French tole urn on top of an Irish console table is filled with a huge bouquet of flowers every Friday to welcome guests. The 19th-century American mirror fills the wall from tabletop to cornice and seems to stretch the ceiling height.*

are never really accurate and if you go back and ask for another gallon, the two batches don't match. I knew there was no way I was going to be able to do this myself, so I hired a young artist I knew to help. He managed to mix up enough gallons to do the room. But because there was so much pigment in the paint and it wasn't really stirred properly, there are places on the wall where you see a little more red, and others where there's a little more yellow. And to me, that makes it all the more beautiful. The room seems to change color all the time, with the shifting light. I could never duplicate it even if I tried because it was completely fortuitous.

Furnishing the living room was not quite as difficult. It's an 18-foot-square room with four French doors and two other entrances, which means a lot of traffic and no wall space for a sofa. So the sofa is in front of the French doors, facing the fireplace. Right next to it is a big overstuffed chair covered in a brown-and-green linen print, where I love to sit with the morning newspapers and the sun pouring in on my shoulders. I arranged the rest of the room for conversation. It had to be just one group because the room is not big enough for two.

To the left of the fireplace against the wall, I placed a 19th-century oak secretary that I bought off the back of a truck in a nearby town. It had a certain style, but I always intended to replace it as soon as I found something really special. Many years later, when one of my favorite antiques dealers, Arnie Schless, decided to move back to Sweden and put his whole shop on sale at Sotheby's, I found an 18th-century Swedish mahogany secretary that was exactly what I had envisioned for this room. Now I have a desk that I really love, along with the added pleasure of remembering Arnie and all I learned from him every time I use it. The sofa is still there, facing the fireplace. It's just that the things around it have gotten better.

Usually the most important space in the house is given over to the living room, but people seldom set foot in it because there's nothing to do there. That's why I happen to like desks in a living room, with pencils and stationery and a phone. If there's no desk or stereo or TV, you're never going to use that space. I think we have this misguided notion that a living room should look a certain way, perfect and pristine, but that kind of untouchability can be soulless. When a room is lived in, you can feel it. The furniture is not stiff and tight, the cushions have molded to the curves of the human body. It feels good to sit there. The room is comforting, and lures you in to cozy up with friends or a good book.

OPPOSITE: *The morning light streams in through tall French doors in the living room. Instead of restricting myself to one period of furniture, I like to combine various styles, which gives a room a relaxed quality. All you need is one strong piece—like this 18th-century Italian carved and gilded mirror—and then the rest can be very simple.*

ABOVE: *One of my favorite pieces is this 19th-century Russian table, gessoed and painted white and gold. It still has its original faux-marble top, done with black paint on canvas.*

OPPOSITE: *A large-scale object—like this aubergine hurricane candlestick on a Japanese black lacquer coffee table—immediately catches the eye and adds stature and excitement to a room.*

LEFT: *A Biedermeier étagère holds an Italian ceramic obelisk flanked by a treasured pair of silk hyacinths protected by glass domes.* ABOVE: *I'll often collect objects in one color and then group them together. Here, white porcelain and faux-ivory are set off with silver.* OPPOSITE: *An unusual marble urn stands in front of a 19th-century mezzotint of rabbits.*

Most people are afraid of scale. They're reluctant to put a big piece of furniture in a small room. But I'll often choose a large-scale sofa and at least one big chair, and then balance them with smaller objects. The general rule is, the bolder the scale, the more interesting the room

LEFT: *The 18th-century Swedish mahogany secretary just to the left of the original 1840 fireplace once belonged to one of my favorite antiques dealers, Arnie Schless. Various benches and chairs, including an 18th-century wing chair in its gently faded original needlepoint, are grouped around the fireplace for easy conversation.*

ABOVE: *A 19th-century bronze whippet, just one of our many dog-related possessions, rests on a marble tabletop.* OPPOSITE: *The English Regency mirror over the mantel is a fine example of verre églomisé—the delicate art of painting and gilding the underside of glass. I chose the flowers to echo the color of the walls. Bouquets of ranunculus are arranged in Worcester cachepots, alternating with French Aptware vases.*

Now that I had all these big, beautiful rooms just waiting for furniture, I had the perfect justification for attending every tag sale, estate sale, and country auction within driving distance. Years ago, when someone died, the family didn't bother to call in an appraiser to go through the contents of the house. They just held a house sale. These were my best sources for everything from pots and pans to embroidered bed linens. I remember buying two dozen down pillows covered in old heavy ticking for $20, and I still have them on my bed. With a good eye, you could find wonderful things. At a country auction, I spotted a set of original Robert Thornton botanical engravings. I didn't think I could afford the half-dozen, so I arranged to buy them with a friend. I think we got all six for $300. When the last lot was sold, the auctioneer came over to me and asked curiously, "What were those prints you bought?" I still have them hanging in my entrance hall. Years later I found two others, but this time the price was much, much more.

When I started out as a designer, one of my greatest joys was spending the whole day in a car, driving around and shopping. I believe you should buy what you can afford and you should have the pleasure of looking for it. Every time you walk into an antiques shop, you're going to learn something. Because I've had the luxury of frequenting very good dealers, I've developed a very good eye and a broad knowledge of furniture. My first job was for the renowned English antiques shop Stair & Co., where I had to write the descriptive tags for incoming shipments. I learned the difference between Sheraton and Hepplewhite, Spode and Rockingham. It was an education in quality.

But it's also rewarding to go into junk shops. For years, John has been a habitué of the Third Avenue thrift stores. He can unearth the most beautiful pair of candlesticks and pull the one piece of Chinese export from a stack of undistinguished plates. I have to admit there's something thrilling in the quest. Anyone can walk into the finest shop run by a great connoisseur and buy a masterpiece. The real challenge is to walk into some poky little place and find something that's stylish or rare.

Albert Hadley was the champion of the unexpected find. When I left Parish-Hadley to go out on my own, he gave me a wonderful chintz-covered chair that is one of my most treasured possessions. It used to be in the living room and now it's my favorite spot to sit in the kitchen. I move things around, which gives me a chance to see them differently. Gradually, I have replaced much of the furniture bought at tag sales or secondhand shops with better pieces. Each year, I try to buy one good painting or one good piece of furniture instead of frittering my money away on lots of little items. You can keep adding and layering up to a point, but if you go too far a room quickly feels cluttered.

A house should evolve over time. As a professional, I know that furnishing a home takes patience and passion. When I'm working with clients, I soon figure out who has the collecting bug. Those who do not should not be forced into appearing as if they do. I think it is wrong to burden people with objects that mean nothing to them. Your home must always reflect who you are, and a good designer will make the effort to bring out a client's character.

John and I are inveterate collectors who relish the hunt, and you can see that in our rooms. There is so much pleasure to be had in learning about the decorative arts. Then, in some out-of-the-way shop in some foreign city, you may discover a treasure that you love, not only for its beauty but because it brings back the day you found it.

OPPOSITE: *The desk in the living room, where I often work, is home to some of my favorite possessions, like a French metal sunflower and a little bronze rabbit by French sculptor Jean-August Barré.*

I like to surround myself with small things that bring back special memories when I sit down at my desk

THE LIBRARY

The only possessions I can't live without are my books, which is why the library took precedence over the living room. The room I chose was a very awkward space, long and narrow, with six doors and two windows. Nothing lined up, which is a nightmare for anyone who loves symmetry, as I do. The one good feature was a large fireplace with a columned mantel. After sitting on the floor and surveying this sad, empty room, I decided that each end needed floor-to-ceiling bookcases—not only to house my large collection of books, but also to make the space seem less long. I added a crown molding to draw attention to the higher ceiling (this room was an 1840 addition to the original 18th-century farmhouse).

Then I had to figure out how to arrange the furniture. Normally, I would put a sofa across from the fireplace, but that didn't work here, so I started over. Often you get a more interesting plan if you let the room tell you where each piece of furniture should be, rather than follow some preconceived notion. In this room, the only place to put the sofa was against one of the long walls, off-center with the fireplace. This meant that all the rest of the chairs needed to make a conversational group were stuck at one end of the room, while the other end risked becoming a mere passage. In order to balance that cluster of furniture but not block the traffic flow, I placed a large center table at the empty end of the room, stacked it with books and magazines, and topped it with a large urn—just waiting to be filled with flowers. There's something so luxurious about a big round table piled with all kinds of tempting books. Most people feel hesitant to go to someone else's shelf and pull down a volume, but they will happily pick one up from a table.

I painted the walls—and all of the trim—the soft beige of a paper bag. Contrasting colors would have only accentuated the room's awkward proportions. But I couldn't resist painting the insides of the two bookcases a dark Chinese red, and the two tall windows are hung with beige-and-red striped curtains. What I learned from this room is that symmetry can be predictable and even boring, whereas asymmetry—if done correctly so that things balance out—is much more intriguing. A three-paneled screen hides an awkward door, behind a wing chair. This was my father's favorite chair, and I can still see him sitting there, with his beautiful long hands resting on its arms. One of the joys of living in a house for a long time are the memories that come to mind from room to room. This house has a past as well as a future.

OPPOSITE: *Sitting by a blazing fire in the library with a good book is my idea of bliss. An early 20th-century American landscape hangs over the mantel, behind the English lusterware pitchers.*

ABOVE: *I love the graceful lines of this 19th-century English painted chair, even though the Prince of Wales plume is missing one feather.* OPPOSITE: *A portrait of an unknown English gentleman was improved by placing it in an antique gilded frame. The English Regency bench makes an elegant coffee table.*

I love sitting in the quiet calm of the library,

with all these great minds as companions

COLLECTING ART

Art history was always my favorite subject in school. For years, I also took drawing and painting classes, until I realized that I would never be more than a mediocre artist. However, the courses opened my eyes and taught me to love art.

I enjoy looking at paintings, drawings, works on paper, or sculpture and would be thrilled to own really great art, but my collecting has been done on a modest budget. Most of my pictures would be classified as merely decorative, but that's all right with me. John and I buy pieces that mean something to us, without worrying about their provenance or whether they will greatly increase in value. We both love early 20th-century American painting and wish we could own one of those luminous, intimate still lifes by Fairfield Porter. But instead we'll search out wonderful pictures by lesser-known artists who still have something inter-esting to say about space and color and light.

Whenever we go shopping, we are always looking for art as well as furniture. In fact, most of our favorite paintings were found in shops that did not specialize in art, but happened to have one particular picture that we couldn't resist. Our taste in art is as eclectic as our taste in furniture. We like many different periods and have great fun mixing things up—an 18th-century landscape might hang next to a contemporary drawing.

For us, our response to a painting is far more important than the signature on the canvas. However, if you are just starting out and wish to buy pictures as an investment, it's a good idea to find a knowledgeable art dealer or consultant who can advise you. Go to galleries and shows and get to know the dealers. They can often find pictures for you if you tell them exactly what you're interested in.

One thing I do know is that an art collection, whether serious or simply decorative, is what makes a home unique. It's a quick glimpse into a person's passion and character. Funnily enough, I have to admit that even if one day I did win the lottery and could buy anything I wanted, I would have a hard time giving up some of the little pictures John and I found along the way. They will always be my treasures.

LEFT: *A collection of 19th-century silhouette pictures is grouped together on the powder room walls.* RIGHT: *I upgraded to a much better portrait of another English landowner and hung it over the library sofa. He is surrounded by various paintings of dogs, acquired on our travels.*

LIVING WITH BOOKS

One is never alone when surrounded by books. To jump into the pages of an exciting mystery, to escape into the past (which always seems to resemble the present in so many ways), to study beautiful images of gardens (and read about someone else's trials and tribulations, as well as triumphs) gives me hours of pleasure. Poring over design books with lavish pictures of houses from all over the world inspires me for the projects ahead.

A library also means you have the fun of assembling a collection of books. Even though the Internet has made this very easy, I still enjoy a great bookstore even more. Sadly, these are getting harder to find, but what a treat to have a book put into your hands by a storeowner who knows you well, and is convinced it would be perfect for you.

Needless to say, I never have enough room for my books. Always build as many shelves as you can—eventually you'll fill them. I arrange my books according to subject so I can retrieve them more easily, but they're not necessarily alphabetical. Instead I'll group them visually by height, so I can fit in a few more, horizontally, on top of the short ones. Leave a little space on each shelf—by starting out with one or two horizontal stacks, for example—so you can make room for newcomers without having to rearrange everything.

I can spend an evening with Thomas Jefferson or Vita Sackville-West, in the company of their books

LEFT: *In the library, I work at this 18th-century English mahogany pedestal desk, with its original red leather top, that I found at auction.* OPPOSITE: *This doorway spans a century, since it leads from the 1840 addition to the original 18th-century heart of the house.*

THE DINING ROOM

The dining room was once the living room of the original 18th-century house, which consisted of this room and a kitchen on the ground floor, with an attached carriage house. The old floorboards show where a small staircase formerly went up to a sleeping loft. When Mr. Brewster added onto the house in the 19th century, I surmise that he replaced a simple Colonial mantel with a grander Federal model. He must have known we were going to live here, because it is much more my style.

The ceilings are lower in this part of the house, and I decided striped wallpaper would add a little height. I ordered a nice green-and-white Federal-style stripe from the venerable wallpaper company, Nancy McClelland—known for her historic patterns all handblocked on real paper. Since I was trying to save money and have always been very good with my hands, I thought I could hang it myself. I had, of course, seen it done many times on my decorating projects and it seemed so simple. I should have remembered that figure skating looks easy when done by a professional.

One Saturday, I talked my friend Alan Campbell into helping me. His business was designing and painting wallpapers and fabrics, so surely he would know what to do. Alas, he confessed that he had never hung wallpaper in his life. Still, he's an artist and I'm supposed to be creative. So, armed with wheat paste, razor blades, and a wallpaper table, we set up in the dining room.

While the strains of Richard Straus's glorious opera, Der Rosenkavalier, floated through the house, we measured the walls, cut the strips and applied the paste. But as soon as we got a strip up on the wall and went to slice off the selvage from the top and bottom edges, the wet paper just fell apart. Eventually, we were surgically trimming each piece with my tiny embroidery scissors.

By the end of the day, after several glasses of wine and dozens of patches, we were covered head to foot in wheat paste and vowing never to do that again. But we did manage to get the wallpaper up, and I gained a new respect for paperhangers.

OPPOSITE: *In the dining room, a green-and-white historic wallpaper provides a proper backdrop for a collection of Regency portraits, done in profile. All the trim in the room, including the mantel, is painted dark green to match the stripe. The mantel holds various candlesticks and a pair of polychrome Delft jars.*

LEFT: *When I met John, I acquired a new appreciation for chickens. Here, a blanc de chine porcelain rooster struts regally in front of a 19th-century French oil painting of a cockerel and his harem.*

OPPOSITE: *The dining table takes on a different look with various pieces of blue-and-white Canton china— some old, some new—on an Indian cotton cloth.*

SETTING THE TABLE

I can set a table in a few minutes flat. Of course it helps if you have the right linens and things, but that doesn't necessarily mean they have to be fancy. I have a round table in my dining room, and it's hard to find round tablecloths. But I've discovered that a king-size bedspread works just fine, and half my tablecloths are inexpensive bedspreads from India. I also never fail to check out the antique textile dealers when I'm at a fair.

Having enough china has never been a problem. I don't know where my love for china started, but I admit I'm addicted to beautiful dishes. You probably eat off your own china twice a day, and who wants to look at the same plate 365 days a year? I could set a table every hour, I enjoy it so much. I think of it as creating a still life with china, glassware, silver—and then you have the challenge of what to put in the middle. I like to have a selection of props to work with—little carved figures or a collection of miniature wheelbarrows that look lovely with berries in them. For my birthday, I set out all sorts of rabbits made of everything from bronze to porcelain. In winter, when I don't have fresh flowers from the garden, I might bring in succulents from the greenhouse. It's interesting to do something a little different from the conventional bouquet. I'm inspired by people like Pauline de Rothschild, who once put a huge wooden carousel horse in the center of a long table set for 20, with flowers in low ramekins down the middle.

My house came with one floor-to-ceiling pantry, but since then I've built two more. They're all full, which means something old has to come out before something new goes in. I justify my china obsession this way: if you're always trying to think of different ways to decorate the table, then obviously you need a lot of options. I might be disciplined and choose plates that are all of a kind—perhaps French porcelain with peach borders—or I might mix things up.

The possibilities expand if you collect china by color. You might make it a point to buy only red and white china, or red and gold, or just pieces with some sort of red in them—then red becomes the unifying element. It doesn't matter if each set of plates has a different pattern; they are all variations on the same theme. Any combination of plates would work well together. Then you might add red cut-glass goblets to complete the scheme.

In the country, I have a little bit of everything. For breakfast in the dining room, I might choose the old-fashioned Napoleonic ivy leaf which Wedgwood copied—white plates with a green ivy border. If we're eating in the kitchen, I might pull out some pottery we bought in Portugal, simple off-white plates with little purple and yellow brushstrokes around the edge. In the conservatory, where we eat a lot, I like to use a set of antique faience with green leaves and little yellow flowers that John found at auction. It's very fragile and chips easily, but I refuse to keep it hidden away. My mother loved china too, and she would buy a teapot she coveted even if it had a hairline crack. She didn't mind if a piece was not absolutely perfect, and I've inherited that sensibility. I believe in using my china, which means it won't stay perfect for long.

Sometimes I get started on a new collection. At a recent tag sale, I spotted some old lusterware with a leaf border—there's something about leaves that I can't resist. There were a dozen dinner plates in a purplish color, which meant I had to look for first-course plates and dessert plates to go with it, for those purple moments. I always try to buy at least twelve of each. I don't own full sets of china, complete with five-piece place settings and all the various serving pieces like gravy boats and sugar bowls. Instead, I prefer to create my own uniquely mismatched service.

This always results in a more interesting dinner table, because the guests do not get bored with the same plate after plate. Each course sets a whole new tone, which makes for a much livelier meal.

OPPOSITE: *I took my cue from the peach-banded French porcelain and picked up the color with small bouquets of marigolds and a large amber crystal tureen filled with lemons. The tiny silver pagodas serve as peppershakers.*

Candles can make even the simplest meal magical—lower the lights to up the atmosphere

Having everything you need on hand

All my china and glassware is neatly stacked behind floor-to-ceiling glass doors, lit from within so I can see everything clearly. Then I just have to decide which combination of plates and cups to put together. OPPOSITE: *A storage closet holds everything else I need for the table—from linens to candles—all in one place. I've found the best way to store tablecloths is on large, open-sided coat hangers.*

makes setting the table a simple endeavor

THE KITCHEN

When I first saw the kitchen, I was shocked. How anyone could cook a meal or even eat a meal in here was beyond me. This one small space had five doors and three windows, which left little room for anything else. The beautiful old fireplace came with a big, gaping hole in the chimneypiece, inexplicably hung with paper fish—an idea that I must confess would never have occurred to me.

In order to fit in a few appliances, I had to find more wall space, which meant reconfiguring the room. By reworking the back staircase so it landed in a different spot and closing off an extraneous exterior door, I managed to free up one wall that was just long enough to hold a new sink, stove, dishwasher, and refrigerator. I pulled up the ugly 1950s vinyl flooring and replaced it with old pine floorboards that we painted with big beige and white diamonds and squares. We put in solid wood cabinetry and spent months stripping layers of paint off the old pine mantel. The fireplace was very plain and simple, with the original baking oven on one side. (Of course, I couldn't wait to brick up the fish tank.)

There was only one feature in the kitchen I didn't want to change. In the center of the room stood a huge worktable made of solid butcher block, probably 80 years old. Endless cooking and baking had burnished the thick, heavy top to a warm honey color. Three deep drawers could hold all sorts of utensils.

I was so excited when we realized, just as we were about to close on the house, that the previous owners would have to leave it for us. The table had clearly been constructed in the room because there was no way to get it out without chopping it in two. I sanded it down, scrubbed it clean and oiled it, and it's still standing in exactly the same spot. When we turn around from the stove or refrigerator or sink, we have this big island to work on. The plan proves how efficient a small kitchen can be. John can easily prepare a meal for 25 people in a relatively tight space.

He is definitely the chef at Manor House. Though I love to cook and am quite proficient at it, I can't do it when he's

OPPOSITE: *Charlie, my beloved adopted mutt, sits on a chair in the kitchen in front of the massive 18th-century fireplace. Painted floors are a New England tradition, and I spruced up these old pine floorboards with a classic checkerboard design. Portuguese pottery adorns the walls and worktable.*

around. John doesn't like to share his kitchen with anyone else. This is his domain. If I want to experiment with a new dessert, I have to wait until he's out at Agway and then seize the moment.

Once, 30 years ago, when the whole house, including the kitchen, was under construction, I found myself with an unexpected houseguest. Van Day Truex, a man of extraordinary taste and refinement, the dean of Parsons School of Design and the creative director of Tiffany's, was househunting in the area and disdained the local inn. Impulsively, I invited him to stay with me for a weekend. On Sunday morning, over a cup of coffee in the makeshift kitchen, he suddenly made a grand sweep of his arm and asked, "Now, what do you plan to do with this room?" I saw his gimlet eye take in the mess and said, "I was thinking of painting it red." He looked at me in horror. "That's the worst color you could ever choose. A kitchen should be white."

So I've always kept it white, in homage to Van Day Truex. A few years ago, John and I decided to push out a wall and square off the room with a bank of windows overlooking the garden. That gave us enough space for a seating area with a table and a French leather bench—a wonderful place to read the paper in the morning, as long as you can get the dogs off it. They love to sit there and bark at the squirrels. It's their version of TV.

RIGHT: *The one major change I made in the old house was to expand the kitchen and add these large, lovely windows overlooking the garden. Now we have room for a breakfast table, which I've surrounded with light and airy Italian cane chairs.*

The kitchen table is set for lunch with 19th-century English creamware plates and handblown Mexican glasses. OPPOSITE: I chose hydrangeas and passionflowers for the table to pick up the purple of the glasses. The lovely blue-and-white gravy boats are filled with gooseberries.

Once, at a party in the country, I found myself inviting some out-of-towners over to see my house the next day. Well, my guests arrived at 11:00 AM absolutely starving since they had not eaten breakfast. I had just planned to introduce them to a few friends over coffee, since their schedule was so tight. But all of a sudden I had twelve people for lunch and I was completely unprepared. While everyone was wandering around looking at the house, I went into the kitchen and had a quiet heart attack. I looked in the larder and said to myself, this is really going to be a loaves-and-fishes number. There was barely any food in the house.

I rummaged around and found a couple pounds of hamburger in the refrigerator, two cans of tomato sauce, and two boxes of linguine pasta. Even more embarrassing—the out-of-towners were Italian! I added garlic, onion, and fresh herbs from my pots by the kitchen window. I was able to stretch it out and make a fairly decent meat sauce for the pasta, and I had just enough salad for everybody to have a lettuce leaf and a sliver of endive. Luckily, I always have vanilla ice cream in the freezer. I put a scoop in a bowl for each person, and then I did my little trick. Sprinkle a spoonful of fresh-ground coffee, a little coarse, on top, and then pour any sort of liqueur, like Grand Marnier, over it. Delicious.

And nobody knew the impromptu lunch wasn't easy as pie (I think it helped that I had plenty of wine in the house). Once this happens to you, you realize you never want it to happen again. Now the larder is always full. The freezer is stocked with cheese straws (that's my Southern heritage) and little sausage biscuits for cocktails if anyone shows up unannounced.

Our motto is, be prepared. If John's cooking lasagna, he'll make two—one for the freezer. There's always something good—like shepherd's pie—in there. Soups freeze beautifully. I also keep at least one box of Duncan Hines double-chocolate brownie mix on hand. You can make them at the last minute, cut them up and serve them on a pretty plate.

What I've learned is that entertaining is sort of like exercise. The more you do it, the easier it is and the better you get at it. I'm amazed how panicked people are at the thought of having people over for dinner, and I'm convinced it's just because they don't do it often enough. John and I are comfortable entertaining because we do it all the time, and if you feel comfortable, so will your guests. Don't make a dinner party into a production, thinking you have to spend a week cleaning the house and then an agonizing three days in the kitchen. Sometimes simple is better—there's nothing finer than a great meat loaf, as our friends will testify. You may serve it on 18th-century china if you like or dishes from K-Mart. The point is to serve it with confidence and pride.

BREAKFAST

On Sundays, we often have a late, hearty brunch with eggs, bacon, and John's special pancakes. (Buy several copies of the Sunday papers so everyone can read their favorite section over coffee.) This is usually enough to keep everyone fortified for the trip home.

John's Pancakes
Makes fourteen 3 1/2 to 4-inch pancakes

1 1/2 cups all-purpose flour
1 teaspoon salt
2 tablespoons granulated white sugar
2 teaspoons double-action baking powder
2 eggs, lightly beaten
3 tablespoons vegetable oil
1 1/2 cups milk
1 teaspoon pure vanilla extract
Dash of salt
Butter and maple syrup for serving

In a large bowl, sift together the flour, salt, sugar, and baking powder. Set aside. In a second large bowl, beat together the eggs, vegetable oil, milk, vanilla, and salt. Fold the flour mixture into the batter.

Heat a large non-stick frying pan. Use a 1/4 cup measure to ladle the batter into the medium hot pan. When small bubbles form on the top of the pancakes, and the bottoms are golden brown, turn them and cook until browned on the other side. Keep warm, and repeat until batter is used up. Serve with butter and maple syrup.

ACCOMPANIMENTS
▪ A selection of cereals
   (Total is my favorite)
▪ Fresh fruit
▪ Good bread for toast
▪ Homemade jams
▪ Coffee and tea

LUNCH

Tomato and Sausage Soup
Serves 4

Four links (about 1 pound) spicy Italian sausages
1 tablespoon olive oil
1 large can whole tomatoes
   (preferably San Marzano)
1 cup water
1 teaspoon dried basil
1/2 teaspoon salt
1/2 teaspoon freshly ground pepper
2 medium zucchini, sliced into rounds,
   ends discarded
Parmesan cheese, grated

Remove sausages from casings. Heat oil in a heavy bottomed soup pan. Add the sausage in a single layer and over a medium heat brown well all over. Add tomatoes, water, and seasoning, mashing tomatoes to break them up. Cover and bring to a boil. Then simmer for 30 minutes. Add zucchini rounds to soup and cook until tender, about 5 minutes. Serve in large soup bowls. Sprinkle Parmesan cheese on top.

NOTE: This soup makes a quick, delicious meal if you keep cans of tomatoes in the pantry and a package of Italian sausage in the freezer. Serve with French bread and a mixed green salad.

LIVING WITH DOGS

Sometimes I think I would rather live with dogs than people (if you have dogs in your life, you'll know what I mean). But not everyone is going to love your dogs as you do. Luckily, there are ways to keep the house looking neat and tidy while your pets make themselves at home.

Needless to say, it's essential to keep your dogs clean. If you live in the country, make sure you have a short hose by the door so you can rinse off the dogs when they have rolled in something unmentionable. Some people never let their dogs on the furniture. I'm not that strict, but I do keep an assortment of throws to wrap around the cushions of a chair or sofa. They help protect the upholstery and can also be taken off and cleaned. If you want a dog to stay off the furniture, provide him with his own comfortable bed. My favorite is the Wally bed from Max Enterprises in Austin, Texas, in faux leopard-skin. Animal prints look good in almost any setting and the cover comes right off so you can throw it in the washing machine. I also keep some woven rush baskets, with cushions, down at the pool house for them.

Of course, dogs have to eat and there's no reason why they shouldn't dine out of something visually pleasing. I use a stainless steel bowl with a rubber ring around the bottom so it doesn't fly all over the floor. They also wash and stack easily. Keep an eye out for interesting water bowls. Often, you can buy an old tureen that's missing its lid very inexpensively.

Store their food in good-looking galvanized stainless steel containers with tight lids. I keep medicine, shampoos, brushes, and combs in a big basket in the cupboard so they're not scattered all over the place. Dedicate one special spot to leashes and collars, so you're not continually searching for them. Hang them neatly on a special rack by the door, drop them into an old umbrella stand, or round them up and tuck them into a basket.

THE MASTER BEDROOM

The choice of which room should be the master bedroom was not immediately clear. Old houses like mine tend to ramble a bit as various rooms are added on over the years. Often, there is no cohesive floor plan. Upstairs, I had to walk through one of the bedrooms to get to another. (I ended up making the first bedroom smaller so I could fit in a hallway.) Across the back of the house was that lovely two-story lattice porch that overlooked what would eventually be the formal garden, and I wanted to sleep in a room that opened onto it.

Unfortunately, there was no access to the porch from the room with the best view, but that didn't stop me. I turned one window into a French door, and now, as soon as the birds wake me up in the morning, I can step out and see my flower beds. In summer, the porch is delightfully cool, shaded by a 250-year-old sugar maple tree so close it makes me feel as if I'm sleeping in a treehouse. I have rocking chairs and a table out there, and sometimes at night before I go to sleep I sit outside and listen to the crickets. Every spring, a bird builds a nest in the lattice right out-side my bedroom door. For almost 30 years, I've been waiting for someone to bring breakfast to me out on this porch. It hasn't happened yet. Still, I'm forever hopeful.

The way our bedroom looks now isn't the way it looked in the beginning. For its first incarnation, I had fallen in love with a flower print chintz on a brown background (apparently no one else did, since I was able to buy it for half-price). I made it into curtains, but as time went on, I decided the fabric was too busy. It stopped the eye, so I replaced it with a handblocked French blue-and-beige Arts & Crafts pattern by my friend Robert Kime in England. I think French blue is a very calming color, and I love it in the daytime with the sun pouring in.

The furniture in the room is a great mix—an American bed, an English chest, a Victorian chair, a tall Directoire bookcase

OPPOSITE: *This beautiful American maple four-poster bed just fit into the master bedroom, practically scraping the ceiling. I hung it with hand-embroidered Indian cotton, backed with cheerful gingham. I love to read in bed, and there's something so cozy about having two good reading lamps inside the bed curtains. There must be a dozen different patterns in this room—from the French Aubusson carpet to the American quilt—but they all work together to create a soft, flowery blur.*

that I found in the south of France, and a black lacquered corner cupboard to hold the TV. I don't worry if the pieces in a room come from all different countries and periods. There are no real rules when it comes to combining things. But for me, the process is rather like making a painting. You have to step back and look at your combinations to see if they complement each other— something simple with something more ornate, something dark next to something light. It's often trial and error, but what I try to achieve is a sense of harmony and balance as I compose small, exciting still lifes within the larger picture of the room.

It always seems to work if I just put things that I like together. I love special beds, and when a friend found a fabulous tiger maple four-poster for me several years ago, I decided it deserved a hand-embroidered cotton from India for the bed hangings. Not much else in the room has changed. One of my favorite pieces is an 18th-century English chest of drawers painted with delicate flowers in the style of Angelica Kaufman, a well-known decorative artist. I bought it at auction for a very reasonable price because someone had added very ugly legs to it. I just took them off and fitted the original chest with a proper bracket base and it now occupies a place of honor in the bedroom.

My collection of needlework pictures portraying flowers, animals, and birds hangs on the walls. (I am always amazed that women once had the time, patience, and skill to produce these exquisite works—something so far removed from my busy life.)

There is nothing too formal here, nothing that couldn't be found in a typical country house. The only real link between the furnishings is that I love them all.

ABOVE: *The master bath was enlarged by relocating the tub to an adjacent closet. I papered the walls above the original wainscoting with a French floral print.* OPPOSITE: *A 19th-century Italian painted desk works nicely as a dressing table, with drawers for cosmetics and a hair dryer. I added the swiveling silver mirror. The bedroom curtains are made from handblocked cotton by Robert Kime.*

ABOVE: *In a guest bath, I papered the walls with a handblocked blue-and-white print and draped an old chintz curtain over a rod, for an instant valance. Then I cut up a sweet, embroidered sheet that had seen better days and made half-curtains.* RIGHT: *Patterns in a guest bedroom—ranging from toile on the curtains to stripes on the mirror—create an enveloping effect. The walls are hung with a collection of bird prints. Old-fashioned dark green roller shades can fend off the early morning sun for late sleepers.*

The Porches

THE PORCHES

There has always been something rather romantic to me about a porch. Growing up in hot, humid Virginia, I spent a lot of time sitting with friends and family on our morning glory-covered porch, the ceiling fans working overtime to cool the air.

Luckily Manor House has many porches, which is probably one of the main reasons why I fell in love with it. Double lattice porches, built to satisfy Mrs. Brewster's longing for her Southern roots, once wrapped several sides of the house. Now only one remains, at the back. Along the south side of the house, the upper level of the porch was removed at some point and the lower portion was screened-in. It's a very long and narrow space, stretching across the living room and library. I was happy to find a nine-foot-long Chesterfield sofa—perfect for napping—to go against one wall. I added lots of wicker chairs and

OPPOSITE: *Languidly curved wicker chaises, a pillow-strewn sofa, and an Irish painted chair all invite guests to linger on the screened porch. Sturdy rush mats help to break up the length of the room and add a summery feeling. All the various shades of green on the painted chairs and the upholstery fabrics lead the eye out to the garden beyond. I love the tole table, striped almost like a circus tent.*

chaises and put a round table at one end, where I can seat four for a summer lunch. On a glorious summer day, who wants to be cooped up in the house?

There's a special quality to the light on a screened porch—softer, gentler, more mysterious. I can settle in with a novel by Eudora Welty or William Faulkner—their characters *lived* on the porch—and read in blissful comfort, even though the sun is blazing. Yet I still feel as if I'm outside. After dinner, John and I will often linger here for hours with a glass of good wine. There will be no lights on, just the candles flickering, as we listen to the cicadas and the peepers and all the other sounds of a summer night. It's quite a symphony.

In winter, the screens come down and the storm windows go up. When snow covers the ground and the sun pours in, the light on the porch is effervescent. The ivies, ferns, and fuchsia plants that hug the shade in summer now lean toward the rays. We'll spend a leisurely morning here with coffee and the Sunday papers and feel warm as toast, even though it's icy cold outside.

LEFT: *Nothing says summer better than a wicker easy chair. These pieces were collected over the years with no particular thought given to matching, although certain things do come in pairs, like the rush-bottomed Irish chairs and the tole tables. The ceiling of the porch is painted sky blue. I've heard that was often done to repel bugs, but that may be an old wives' tale.* ABOVE: *An antique plant stand is laden with ivies, ferns, and herbs.*

ABOVE: *Anyone who loves plants as much as I do needs a good collection of urns. Tucked underneath the plant stand are two birdhouses and a wicker dog carrier.* OPPOSITE: *Who could resist fern-printed pillows? I like to lean back in one of these chaises with a good book and a glass of iced tea on a lazy summer afternoon.*

ABOVE: *At one end of the screened porch, this metal-mesh table with matching chairs is the setting for many light summer lunches.* OPPOSITE: *The flower arrangement comes straight from the garden, with a few stalks of cherry tomatoes tucked in among the nasturtiums and lettuce leaves. The tiny watering cans are actually peppershakers.*

ABOVE: *I bought these topiary yews—which date to 1910—from a grower on Long Island who was going out of business, and planted them in front of the carriage house.* OPPOSITE: *Passionflower vines wend their way along the arched openings where carriages once drove in. Now I've turned this section into a loggia. The reproduction Gothic table holds special plants and some smaller topiaries.*

A good gardener understands plants, and knows just

what should be controlled and what should be left alone

The loggia is another good spot for a summer lunch. A bouquet of dahlias sits on an Indian bedspread, used as a tablecloth. The metal dining chairs were made in France.
OPPOSITE: One of my favorite views of the house is from the porch right off our bedroom, which looks down into the garden.

THE POTTING SHED

At the end of the service wing in the former carriage house, there was a wonderfully rustic space that had probably once been the tack room. It had old pine floors and a long narrow window looking out over the lawn. This room immediately became my potting shed.

Every gardener needs a workspace—for the stacks of clean terra cotta pots awaiting the newest seedlings, for the bins of potting soil and fertilizer, for the tools that need to be close at hand because they're used constantly. Under the window was a long wooden worktable that was perfect for storing pots and mixing the soil to go into them. This room gets a lot of heavy use, but the old pine floors just get better and better as the dirt is swept off after a morning's work.

Under a small window, I placed an old schoolhouse desk where I keep my gardening notebook. Planting dates, blooming dates, and rainfall counts are all recorded for future reference. Successes and failures are documented. The notebook also holds a supply of labels to go into the pots so I can remember what I've planted (this gets harder every year).

Nearby, an old wicker rocker provides the perfect place to sit and read the directions explaining how to treat these tiny plants that I hope, by summer's end, will have grown to be enormous and bursting with blooms.

RIGHT: *In addition to the usual rakes and trowels, the potting shed tends to collect a motley assortment of gardening gear: vintage baskets, stray wooden finials, old wire plant supports with crisscrosses and curlicues that look almost like folk art. There's even a Moroccan lantern hanging from the ceiling, an extra that we haven't yet found room for outside.*

A potting shed is a special place for any gardener; here all sorts of ideas and schemes are hatched

THE

SUNKEN GARDEN

THE SUNKEN GARDEN

If you take the time to listen, the land will speak to you. The idea is to make your garden correspond to fit what nature has already given. In order to understand what you've got to work with, you must thoroughly examine your site, noting all the assets and drawbacks, studying the lay of the land.

Did I do this? Not quite. I couldn't wait to get started. Off to the south of the house, where the sunlight lingers late into the afternoon, the lawn slopes down to a wide, flat area bordered by two lilac hedges. A lovely older lady who lives in the village told me that she used to come to the Brewster house for lawn tennis and iced tea. At either end of the vestigial court, there were a few climbing roses—all that was left of a garden.

My first impulse was to rush right off to the nursery and buy dozens of plants to make a new garden there. I put in the perennial borders first, filling the beds with peonies, iris, and phlox, and built two big lattice fences to go behind them. Of course, I've now had to take out everything I put in because I did it all wrong. I was in too much of a hurry. If you're going to do peren-

nial borders, you have to make them the right way, which means they must be double-dug. You have to dig out the first 18 inches of topsoil, lay it off, and then go down another two feet. You take that subsoil, mix it with manure and nutrients, and put it back. Then you add more topsoil, compost, and manure. By the time you're done, the plants have a footing of very rich soil.

But I did things all backwards. As soon as I put in those first flowerbeds, I realized the garden would be much more exciting if I had a stone wall. Luckily, I knew just the man for the job: my friend Christopher Hewat. He's an artist—a sculptor brought up in New England who's passionate about stone and how it fits together. I bought the stone and he built the wall for me.

The stone wall terraces the land. Now you have the definite sensation of moving from one space to another when you walk down the six big, wide steps that lead to the garden. The flat area

OPPOSITE: *The pool in the center of the sunken garden is painted a natural looking gray-black because the darker the surface, the more reflective it will be. John tends the carp and goldfish. Dwarf Newport Blue boxwood surrounds a flagstone terrace and defines the space, creating the sense of an intimate garden room.*

suddenly feels like a room, bounded by the low stone wall, the lattice behind the perennial borders, and a tall yew hedge.

Many years later, I decided there was too much lawn between the perennial borders—so I built a reflecting pool in the center. I wanted the sound of water, which can make you feel 10° cooler on a sweltering summer day. Around the pool is a stone terrace, bordered with a boxwood hedge. At each corner, we planted tall, cylindrical evergreens that have now reached a height of about 15 feet. It's very important to have something tall in a garden if you want to create the sensation of being protected and enclosed. Subliminally, the evergreens also connect you with the sky and establish a ceiling plane in a virtual room.

Some people may find it comforting to realize that practically everything in this garden has come about through correcting mistakes. Initially, I planted delicate coral bells and other little flowers. But this is the garden John and I see from the screened porch, and those were too small to register from a distance. I switched to plants with leaves the size of platters.

Now I realize that you have to get the scale and structure right before you plant anything. You have to consider views and the relationships between spaces and make a plan that works for the whole site. First, you should study your house and think about how to get yourself to the front door. I always wanted a walkway lined with boxwood—not a hedge this time, but big round shrubs. I started out with measly 12-inch balls that have finally tripled in size. To be a good gardener, you also have to be patient, which is

hard for me. I planted them on either side of a path I made from old brick, so that it would look as if it has always been there.

But it turns out we rarely use the front door. We park closer to the back door, and that's where we bring in the groceries, or head out to the garden and come back laden with flowers. I'm in and out of this door umpteen times a day, and there's no reason why it shouldn't be pleasurable. An enormous 150-year-old maple keeps the area in almost constant shade. When I couldn't get even pachysandra to grow, I knew I was in trouble. So I decided to put up a white picket fence and pave the whole area with flagstones. I planted my garden in pots, experimenting with fuchsia and ferns, which could move out for a spell in the sun and retreat to the greenhouse in winter. After I added a cast-stone table and chairs, it became a wonderful place to sit with coffee and listen to the birds.

When you're doing a plan of your property, always remember that the spaces you leave empty are just as important as the spaces you fill. It is possible to have too much of a good thing—in other words, too many gardens. An expanse of lawn offers serenity and makes a nice contrast to the profusion of flowers. I left the rest of the backyard alone, and simply bordered it with shrubs. The green grass shows off the white clapboard house, and a wide-open lawn also provides the perfect place to put up a tent for a party.

OPPOSITE: *When planning a perennial border, I think about the mixture of leaf textures just as much as flowers. Here, sedum Autumn Joy, allium, sphaerocephalum, phlox, and cimicifuga are some of the plants that combine to create a tapestry effect. Plume poppies give height and structure to the back of the beds.*

The branches of two 80-year-old apple trees had knit together over the years to form a natural arch, which I accentuated with an arched gateway in the tall yew hedge. Just inside the lattice are two benches, where you can sit and hide from the rest of the world. I always like to create a doorway in the garden, to lead you on.

ABOVE: *The stone wall and lattice fences mark the boundaries of the sunken garden. Then the box hedges around the pool create a room within a room.* OPPOSITE: *You need large clumps of plants with interesting leaf textures to carry a border of this size. Hostas and Lady's Mantle form the edges, with old-fashioned roses tumbling over the lattice fence in back.*

If you look closely at your land, it will

tell you where the garden wants to be

THE BARN

A French terra cotta dog sits on the gravel courtyard outside the barn to welcome guests. OPPOSITE: *I wanted the exterior of the renovated barn to still look like a barn, so we found some old-fashioned hardware and put up sliding barn doors. The siding is stained a faded gray-green to blend into the landscape.*

THE BARN

An old red barn, built in 1840, stood on the property. Over the course of years, it had become the garage, filled with garbage cans, storm windows, screens, the tractor, the lawn mower, and anything else I didn't know quite what to do with but still wasn't ready to get rid of. There was a woodworking bench with tools in the back, assorted skis leaning against the walls, and canoes hanging from the ceiling next to various lengths of ladders and poles for pruning the apple trees.

When John came into my life, I would catch him eyeing this building. He would take out the garbage and mentally measure the height of the ceiling—22 feet to the ridgepole. Now the one thing you should know about John is that he really loves big scale. If there's a wall eight feet long, he's going to put a seven-foot-long piece of furniture on it. While I'm saying, "No, no, that won't fit," he goes right ahead and moves it in and lo and behold, it looks terrific. He likes big furniture in large, lofty spaces. But my mainly 19th-century house has small rooms, typical of the period. John kept looking for a great room more suitable to his vision, and finally he found it. One day he came in from a garbage run and announced that we really should turn the barn into one huge room, for entertaining. I went out with him to take another look and thought, that's a great idea. It was also the perfect way to let him have his own space to play with on the property.

We called in an expert on barns to help us figure out how to heat the place without ruining it. Insulation panels needed to be sandwiched into the walls. We chose a Swedish radiant-heat system with pipes coiled under the floor because it was unobtrusive. I was eager to try a concrete floor, and to make it even more interesting we poured it into a grid of old, rough boards. Once a year, it gets polished with butcher's paste wax to enhance the patina.

We built a great big fireplace on the north side of the barn and John found an 1840s mantel and two beautiful arched windows to flank it. On the east side, we jettisoned the 1950s roll-up garage doors in favor of French doors, but had sliding barn doors made for the exterior. That means we can cover the glass, if we want to. This is the main approach to the barn, and we didn't want it to read as another house. In fact, we were so concerned with preserving its character that we ended up practically taking the barn apart board by board and then piecing it back together. At one point, all that was left standing was the hand-hewn post-and-beam frame.

Unfortunately, we had to cut one of those timbers and replace it with steel because we couldn't ask people to crawl over it in order to step into the new guest bedroom (formerly the hayloft). Up here you can really see the beautiful hand-hewn boards on the ceiling. Some of them are easily four feet wide and were known as kingwood, because such majestic wood was once saved for the British monarch.

Luckily John, whom I call the king of beds, had this extraordinary nine-foot-tall Southern plantation bed that could fit nowhere else since the ceilings in the house aren't even eight feet high. The canopy, hung with handblocked Indian cotton patterned with ancient Moghul designs, feels so cozy that everyone clamors to stay here. Nobody has ever complained about not having a good night's sleep in this bed.

Underneath the guest bedroom and bath, we divided the ground floor into a kitchen, powder room, boiler room, and potting shed, saving the bulk of the barn for entertaining. If we had realized how much entertaining we would actually do here, we might have made the kitchen a little larger. But it's amazing how many meals John can produce out of a rather modest space. In keeping with the barn aesthetic, we made grilles out of chicken wire for the upper cabinet doors.

The great big 30- by 50-foot room in the barn was the first space John and I ever decorated together. It's fun to collaborate, particularly when you're working with someone whose taste you share. We often head straight for the same piece of furniture in an antiques shop. If there's a conflict between us, it usually has more to do with quantity than quality. I'm more of an editor, while John is truly a collector and a collector never stops. Just when we've agreed that a room can't possibly hold anything more, all of a sudden something else arrives. It's hard to say no to him, because the newfound object is always so special.

For this huge space, all the furniture had to be of a certain scale, which was no problem for John. At an antiques show, he instinctively gravitates to the biggest mirror or the largest cabinet, while I'm fiddling with a little carved ivory box. Anything strong and bold and masculine instantly appeals to him. The enormous sofa that now stands in the middle of the room was bought at auction for a very reasonable price, since there are not that many rooms that can accommodate a sofa nine feet long and four feet deep. That was our starting point, and then I showed John various pieces that I owned and loved and he showed me his choices. Then we had a tug of war about what was going to go where. Luckily my long French farmhouse table fit perfectly behind the sofa, and he added a marble-topped pedestal table and an early American gateleg table on either side. John found the giant butler's tray, which he had made into a coffee table. (Copies of this piece have since become one of the mainstays of his furniture line.)

In John's shop, there was an Italian sofa covered in its original red linen upholstery with red velvet appliqué, which I admired. It soon made its way to the barn, along with two highbacked Italian chairs, one covered in its original tapestry and the other in leather. Now they stand on either side of the stone-topped table we use as a desk. An English wing chair covered in crewel-work faces the door and is a favorite with our dogs, who like to sit there, waiting for guests.

At first we didn't have a rug. Then a very dear friend who often helps me find beautiful carpets came to dinner and I asked him to let me know if he ever came across a rug that might work. A few days later, a huge bundle arrived at my office. I unwrapped a corner and saw this beautifully faded Persian carpet with scattered beige flowers and knew immediately that this was the perfect rug for the room. We put it down for the winter to add warmth and coziness and then replace it with light and airy sisal in the summer. It's such an old rug that we're hoping it will last twice as long by giving it a yearly rest.

Now that the barn is completed, it has become our social center. We still sleep and breakfast in the main house, but the barn is where we tend to congregate. Because of its size, we can entertain a large group of people comfortably. In winter, we have cocktails around the fire. In summer, we leave the French doors open so the breeze flows through. The large cabinet under the stairs is where we set out the dishes for the buffet dinners we love to give. Twelve people can easily serve themselves and then move on to the conservatory to sit down for dinner. I hate balancing a plate in my lap. Besides, conversation is so much better around a table.

Shopping for the barn with John was such a pleasure that neither of us can bear to let it end. Recently, we couldn't resist some huge watercolors of Rome, done by a friend. There have actually been very few disagreements. There was one lamp at the back of the sofa that I had chosen, and John kept saying, "I really don't like that lamp." One day, when we were packing up to head for the country he just threw another lamp into the car. He turned out to be right—the new acquisition was bigger in scale and better for the room.

Shopping is one of the things John and I do best. Fun for us is going off antiquing in Hudson, New York, for the day, or getting on a plane to the Paris flea market. The problem is we always fall in love with something else. We need nothing. We have no more room for anything. But that doesn't mean you don't spot a wonderful little drawing of a whippet you have to have. It's easier to find a home for something small. But now we have a new rule—something's got to leave before anything else can come in.

On a winter morning, when I'm looking for John, I know exactly where to find him. He will usually be alone in the barn, listening to music—anything from Beethoven to the Brooklyn Tabernacle Choir. Or he might be sitting at the stone-topped desk, talking on the phone to a friend. The barn is his refuge, and his latest triumph.

As you come out of the guest bedroom in the old hayloft, you get an overall view of this enormous space. The lantern hanging from the 22-foot-high ceiling was modeled on one we saw at the Uffizi Gallery in Florence, Italy. OPPOSITE: An early 19th-century English bull's-eye mirror reflects the grandeur of the hand-hewn beams. A pair of carved wooden lions and tiny vases filled with sunflowers flank a portrait of my beloved Brewster.

ABOVE: *John found a pair of tall arched windows at an antiques show, and liked them for their unusual arrangement of panes—the muntins are staggered, instead of evenly aligned. The lamp is made from an old wooden baluster.*
OPPOSITE: *John loves big scale and finally found a room large enough to accommodate it. He uses the Italian marble-topped table as a desk. Behind it is an Italian chair, still with its original needlework and equally imposing.*

When I sit here and look out these beautiful windows,

it's hard to imagine that this room was once a garage

The furniture is grouped around the fireplace, using two sofas and a number of chairs for maximum seating. John's butler's-tray coffee table has the right scale for the room. Then I put a tea table in front of the Italian sofa, for versatility. OPPOSITE: *The Italian sofa is still covered in its original red linen with red velvet appliqué—fraying at the arms, but I don't mind. Pillows made of old textiles invite you to sit down and relax. I threw a paisley shawl over the back to add another layer and break the long line of the sofa.*

ABOVE: *A high table, instead of a low table, in front of a sofa means you can get a lot more use out of your living space. You could even pull up a few chairs and have a meal around it.* OPPOSITE: *I'm always looking for chairs that have a little magic, like this pair of richly carved Spanish Colonial side chairs with distinctive urn-shaped splat backs.*

The rooms that you use on a daily basis are the rooms

people will always want to sit in, because they have soul

COLLECTING TEXTILES

One of the best ways to relax a room and warm up any decor is with textiles. I'm always looking for that special piece of woven, printed, or embroidered material that has great character of its own and can add a little interest to any interior. I'll use these pieces for cushions, to cover a chair, or sometimes I'll just throw something like a beautiful quilt over the back of a sofa. I love to add pattern to a room in this manner, using its richness and complexity to complement the plain upholstery fabrics I prefer on big pieces of furniture.

Unusual textiles can be found in many places. There are normally a few dealers at any antiques fair and now there is eBay, where I have spotted great embroidered suzanis. Old standbys like Pier 1 Imports are still great for handblocked Indian cottons. Be a little creative, and you can find all sorts of uses for old things. Vintage crewel curtains can be relined and made into a throw

to go over the back of a sofa. Scraps of needlework can be made into cushions or used to cover a bench. I love trying to find pieces of furniture still upholstered in their original needlework. This adds a wonderful mellow texture to a room.

When you're using a group of textiles in one room, it's important to have a constant. I usually start with one basic color, and then pick out different textures and patterns. Then I vary the scale of each pattern, choosing perhaps a large floral, a stripe, and then a smaller check. It's hard to mix three large-scale patterns together. You need the contrast that comes with variations on a theme.

Then I might look for a little bit of leather. There's something about the worn, crackled finish of old leather that I find very appealing. Recently, when someone sat down in my beautiful vintage Danish chair and split the leather seat, I looked for someone who could recover it but make it look as old as possible. I've come to learn that age is beautiful. That's why we like old furniture and old houses. Some people want to ignore the past. They think only the future is important. But I think we get to the future by going through the past.

LEFT: *Charlie takes a break. An Indian handblocked quilt covers the cushions of the sofa so the dogs are always welcome.* RIGHT: *We installed a staircase up to the old hayloft and turned it into a guest room. Paintings of farm animals are hung on the far wall.*

The more I know about men, the more I love my dog

Old boards set into polished concrete add patina to the new barn floor. As you can see, the dogs are completely at home here. Chairs like this Danish Modern model and the Spanish beauty with the unusual urn-shaped back add character to the room. A stack of handpainted dishes from India sits on an English oak chair once used in a chapel.

ABOVE: *A bouquet of white dahlias and hydrangea in a silver container picks up on the pale, ethereal palette in the powder room.* OPPOSITE: *The amazing marble sink with Doric columns for legs was in pieces in a box when John spotted it at auction. We covered the walls with beadboard, an appropriate choice for a rustic building.*

A Venetian mirror is not what you would expect to see

in a barn—but that's what makes this room so intriguing

One of the old chestnut beams becomes a
convenient ledge for a collection of topiaries
and succulents under a sunny window in the
guest room. OPPOSITE: The nine-foot-tall
Southern plantation bed, beautifully carved out
of mahogany, is hung with Indian cotton handblocked with ancient Moghul designs. Good
reading lights are tucked in behind the fabric.

In the guest bath, we used old floorboards from the barn to face the tub and turned a lovely old pine chest into a vanity by installing a porcelain sink into its original marble top. OPPOSITE: A round window that we found at an antiques show brings more light into the room. Vintage apothecary jars are arrayed along the beam.

I love the idea
of eating in
different places
around the house.
It breaks the
monotony of
always sitting in
the same seat
in the same room.
Set up a table in
a foyer or a porch,
and you'll get a
whole new perspec-
tive on the room

LEFT: *Queen Anne chairs are pulled up to a festive table, where two ceramic roosters preside over the scene. Over the years, we have managed to collect quite a lot of chicken paraphernalia, and it's fun to use it as part of a place setting.*

When giving a dinner party, I think one of the easiest and most relaxed ways of serving is to present the food on a side table or a buffet. It's lovely to see all the dishes stretched out in abundance, and guests can serve themselves and take exactly what they like. I prefer this to the hustle and bustle of changing courses, which is hard to do seamlessly unless you have servants—and that's not the way we live. Then we pass the platters for those who want a second helping. Guests don't have to get up from the table and the conversation continues uninterrupted.

For the menu, we try to have many choices—a meat, a starch, several vegetables, and a salad. If we sauté one vegetable until tender, we'll usually keep another a little crisper, to add a different texture. It's very important to make each dish look appealing by adding garnishes like fresh herbs around the edges of the platter, or chopped up and scattered over the top. In the garden, I'm continually looking for other edible garnishes like nasturtiums or interesting little lettuce leaves.

When guests arrive at the table, I always have a seating plan. If there are eight people or more, I'll make place cards so everyone knows where to sit. This avoids any awkward moments. I mix my guests up—no couples together—and try to seat people next to someone they know on one side and someone new on the other. If you have a quiet friend, put him or her next to someone who is more outgoing. When you give a little thought to seating your guests, it makes for a more successful party.

Along with carafes of water, we always put several open bottles of wine on the table so guests can help themselves.

Make Entertaining Easy

■ For a simple, savory soup, make a stock out of leftover chicken and bones. Chop up a handful of fresh vegetables—tomatoes, peppers, scallions—and add to strained broth just before serving. Scatter cilantro, parsley, or Parmesan cheese on top for more flavor.

■ If you can't get freshly baked bread, cut pita bread into strips, drizzle with olive oil, and bake in a 300°F oven until crisp.

■ For an easy entrée, season a whole filet of beef (3 to 4 pounds) with salt, pepper, and thyme. Roast in a preheated 450°F oven for 30 minutes. Turn off the oven but leave the meat inside, covered with aluminum foil. An hour and a half later, it will be a nice shade of pink and some tasty juices will have collected in the bottom of the pan.

■ For crisp roasted potatoes, parboil new potatoes for 5 to 7 minutes, until the point of a knife meets no resistance. Meanwhile, preheat a roasting pan, with a little olive oil inside, in a 375°F oven. Drain potatoes well, and crisp in the oven for about 15 minutes. Sprinkle with sea salt.

■ Store-bought ice cream is the basis for many of my desserts, but I always make sure to bring it to room temperature—there's nothing worse than rock-hard ice cream. Serve in a crystal bowl—sprinkled with freshly ground coffee beans or pulverized chocolate and splashed with a little liqueur—for the perfect end to a meal.

Carrot Peanut Soup
Makes 8 half-cup servings

1 pound carrots, peeled and thinly sliced
2 Granny Smith apples, peeled, cored, and coarsely chopped
3 cups chicken broth
2 tablespoons smooth peanut butter
Salt and freshly ground black pepper to taste

Place carrots, apples, and chicken broth in a saucepan. Bring mixture to a boil. Reduce heat, cover pan, and simmer until carrots and apples are soft, about 10 minutes. Place soup in the bowl of a food processor fitted with a steel blade. Process until smooth. Pour soup back into the saucepan, and stir in peanut butter until texture is smooth. Season to taste and gently reheat.

New England Pot Roast
Serves 8

1 teaspoon salt
1/4 teaspoon freshly ground pepper
3 tablespoons all-purpose flour
3 to 4 pounds boned and rolled bottom round pot roast
1/2 cup fresh, grated horseradish or one 4-ounce jar of prepared horseradish, drained
1 cup canned cranberry sauce
1 stick cinnamon, broken in two pieces
4 whole cloves
1/2 cup beef broth
1/2 cup red wine
3 tablespoons bacon drippings or vegetable oil
16 small white onions, peeled
1 bunch carrots, peeled and cut into 3-inch pieces

Stir salt and pepper into the flour and dredge the meat in the mixture, making sure to rub over all surfaces. Mix together horseradish, cranberry sauce, cinnamon, cloves, broth, and wine and set aside.

Heat bacon drippings in a heavy Dutch oven or casserole and brown meat on all sides over high heat. Pour off drippings and reserve. Add horseradish mixture to the meat and bring to the boil. Then cover tightly, lower heat, and simmer for 2 hours.

In the meantime, brown onions and carrots in reserved drippings in the skillet. Add to meat broth, cover again, and cook 25 minutes longer or until vegetables and meat are tender. Serve with buttered noodles.

NOTE: This dish is more flavorful made the night before and re-heated.

Portuguese Drunken Chicken
Serves 4 to 5

3/4 stick (4 tablespoons) unsalted butter
2 tablespoons Dijon mustard
3 medium ripe tomatoes, roughly chopped
10 small white onions, or 3 medium onions, peeled and coarsely chopped
4 garlic cloves, peeled and finely chopped
4 medium-sized carrots, peeled and cut into 1-inch pieces
1/2 cup port wine or sherry
4 cups white wine
8 chicken thighs
4 chicken breasts, excess fat removed

Preheat oven to 375°F. Heat the butter and mustard in a saucepan, whisking until well blended. In a medium bowl, mix the toma-

toes, onions, garlic, carrots, port wine, and white wine together.

Place the chicken pieces in a large casserole or heavy baking dish. Add the butter-mustard mixture to the tomato marinade, and pour the mixture over the chicken pieces. Leave for 2 hours.

Bake the chicken for 1 1/2 hours or until it is tender, basting often with the marinade. Serve immediately.

Cheese Grits Soufflé
Serves 8 to 10

2 1/4 cups milk
2 1/4 cups water
1 cup old-fashioned grits
1 pound coarsely grated cheddar cheese
Salt and freshly ground black pepper to taste
5 eggs, room temperature and separated
Dash of paprika

Preheat oven to 350°F. In a non-stick saucepan, bring milk and water to a boil. Slowly stir in grits. Reduce heat to low and cover pan. Cook grits 12 to 14 minutes or until thickened, stirring occasionally. Remove pan from heat and stir in cheese until thoroughly incorporated. Season with salt and pepper and set aside to cool.

Mix egg yolks together in a medium bowl. Stir into cooled grit mixture. Beat the egg whites in a bowl with an electric mixer until soft peaks form. (Do not overbeat.) Add paprika. Gently fold egg whites into grits mixture.

Spoon mixture into a 9- by 14- by 2-inch ovenproof dish. Bake in the oven for 1 to 1 1/2 hours or until the top is lightly browned and crisp on the edges. Serve immediately.

Orzo with Peas and Parmesan Cheese
Serves 4 to 6

Pinch of salt
1 pound orzo
1 package frozen green peas
2 tablespoons olive oil
3 tablespoons grated Parmesan cheese
1 bunch Italian parsley, coarsely chopped

Bring 4 to 5 quarts of water to a rolling boil. Add salt. Stir the orzo gently in the water and return to heat. Boil uncovered for about 8 minutes, until tender but firm to the bite.

Add peas. Cook 2 minutes until the peas are tender. Remove from heat and drain thoroughly. Transfer to a serving bowl. Stir in olive oil. Add Parmesan cheese and toss. Sprinkle with parsley and toss again.

SETTING UP THE BAR

One way of making your guests feel comfortable is to leave a drinks tray out in plain sight, so you can just say, "Help yourself." On a table, I'll set up a large tray with bottles of the basic liquors and sodas, along with several nice glasses, a silver ice bucket, cocktail napkins, and openers. All you have to do when friends arrive is add ice to the bucket and put out a bottle of chilled white wine.

Stocking the Bar

- Bourbon
- Gin
- Rum
- Scotch
- Vermouth
- Vodka
- Red and white wine
- Ginger ale
- Coke and Diet Coke
- Tonic
- Worcestershire sauce
- V-8 juice or Bloody Mary mix
- Lemons and limes
- Soda water, preferably Perrier or San Pellegrino

Cheddar Cheese Olives
Makes 3 to 4 olives per person

1 2/3 cups unbleached flour
1 teaspoon salt
1/4 teaspoon cayenne pepper
1 stick (8 tablespoons) unsalted butter, cut into bits
8 ounces extra-sharp Cheddar cheese, grated
2 tablespoons iced water
Two 4-ounce jars Spanish green olives stuffed with pimentos, drained

Preheat oven to 350°F. Mix flour, salt, and cayenne. In a food processor, combine dry ingredients with butter and cheese and process until the mixture looks like coarse breadcrumbs. Add water and pulse several times, until the mixture starts to form a ball.

Remove dough from bowl and knead with lightly floured hands. Take 1 teaspoon of dough and enclose each olive. Repeat until all olives are covered. Put the coated olives on a cookie sheet spaced 1/2 inch apart. Cover with plastic wrap and refrigerate for at least 1/2 hour. Bake for 10 to 12 minutes, until the pastry is lightly browned. The cheese olives can also be baked later. After making them, place the cookie sheet in the freezer covered with plastic wrap. When the olives are frozen, transfer to freezer storage bags. Bake for 15 minutes.

One of the easiest and most enjoyable ways of entertaining is to invite friends over for a Sunday afternoon tea. Americans tend to regard afternoon tea as stuffy and old-fashioned, but I like to think of it as a great time for people to get together. Families can drop by after a day in the park. The men can watch a football game if they wish, the ladies can discuss their latest shoe purchases, and the kids can be part of the fun because it's still early in the day. Everything can be done ahead of time so there is much less pressure on the hosts.

John and I prepare lots of tiny tea sandwiches. We always use thin Pepperidge Farm bread to make the sandwiches. Then we cut off the crusts and slice them in half. My favorites are tomato and cucumber, chicken salad with chutney, egg salad, and pimento cheese. And we always have peanut butter and honey for the children.

For dessert, serve brownies (Duncan Hines—my favorite), cookies (made or bought, depending on your time), and possibly a cake. (If you cannot make one, you can order the most delicious caramel cake from Carolyn's Cakes in Richmond, Virginia. They ship all over the country.)

Serve hot tea (or iced tea in the summer), hot cider (or lemonade) for the younger crowd, and always have a beer or two on hand for the husbands, just in case.

I use small plates for the food, and attractive cocktail napkins.

Oatmeal Lace Cookies
Makes 36 cookies

1 1/2 cups rolled oats
3/4 cup dark brown sugar, firmly packed
3/4 cup granulated white sugar
3 tablespoons all-purpose flour
1/4 teaspoon salt
1 egg, lightly beaten
2/3 cup (11 tablespoons) butter, melted
1 teaspoon pure vanilla extract
1/2 cup pecans or walnuts, shelled and finely chopped

Preheat oven to 350°F. Grease two cookie sheets. In a mixing bowl, combine the oats, sugars, flour, and salt. Make a well in the center and add the egg, melted butter, and vanilla. Mix until blended and then stir in chopped nuts. Drop rounded teaspoons of batter, about 2 inches apart, on the cookie sheets. Bake until lightly browned on the edges, about 5 to 8 minutes. Let cookies cool on the cookie sheets for 2 minutes. Transfer to a rack.

ABOVE: *We turned the old workroom in the barn into another potting shed. The wainscoting and open shelves were made of natural, unstained mahogany to withstand all the water.* OPPOSITE: *When we found this old copper butler's sink, we knew exactly where it should go. Foot pedals from a kitchen supply company control the water flow.*

Special thought should be given to the utilitarian spaces

where you spend the most time—make them enjoyable

FLOWER ARRANGEMENTS

When I arrive at the house after a busy week of work in the city, the very first thing I want to do is arrange the flowers for the weekend. There is nothing like fresh flowers to make a room come alive. Whether you have your own garden or buy blossoms from a local market, doing the flowers should not be an overwhelming job.

I am of the simple and natural school of flower arranging—I want my bouquets to look as if Mother Nature made them. I always grow flowers in colors that will complement my interiors—orange, peach and yellow for the living room, dark red for the barn, blue for the bedrooms, cream and white for anywhere and everywhere.

I like small arrangements on tabletops, beside a bed, in the bathroom. I think flowers look best when only one or two colors are used together. Arrangements with too many shades are not as stylish.

Starting with the correct container is a must. I find containers that have a small opening and a larger base—a pitcher, a creamer, even a sugar bowl—lend themselves wonderfully to small bouquets. Matching the color of the flowers to the container completes the picture and creates a charming display.

A beautiful centerpiece gets a dinner party off to a splendid start and makes everyone feel special

LEFT: *It's important to plan the seating in advance. If you've mapped out a good mix of personalities, conversation will flourish.* OPPOSITE: *A bouquet of white snapdragons, hydrangeas, and dahlias—all from the garden—shows how elegant one-color flower arrangements can be. For a dinner table, keep it low so people can still see one another.*

ABOVE: *My collection of vases is neatly arrayed on shelves in the laundry room. I'm convinced you can never have enough containers. With plenty to choose from, you're more likely to find a perfect match for your bouquet.* OPPOSITE: *Flowers, just cut from the garden, rest in buckets of water by the back door so they can have a nice long drink before going into smaller vases.*

Flower arrangements should be made to look as easy and natural as possible. I'll often assemble a small bouquet in my hand, tie it with raffia and then put it into a container. Even in large arrangements, like the one that greets guests in the hall, I want to keep a natural feeling to the plant material—as if you had just come across it in the woods. A beautiful French Aptware urn, filled with hydrangeas, sits on the desk in the barn.

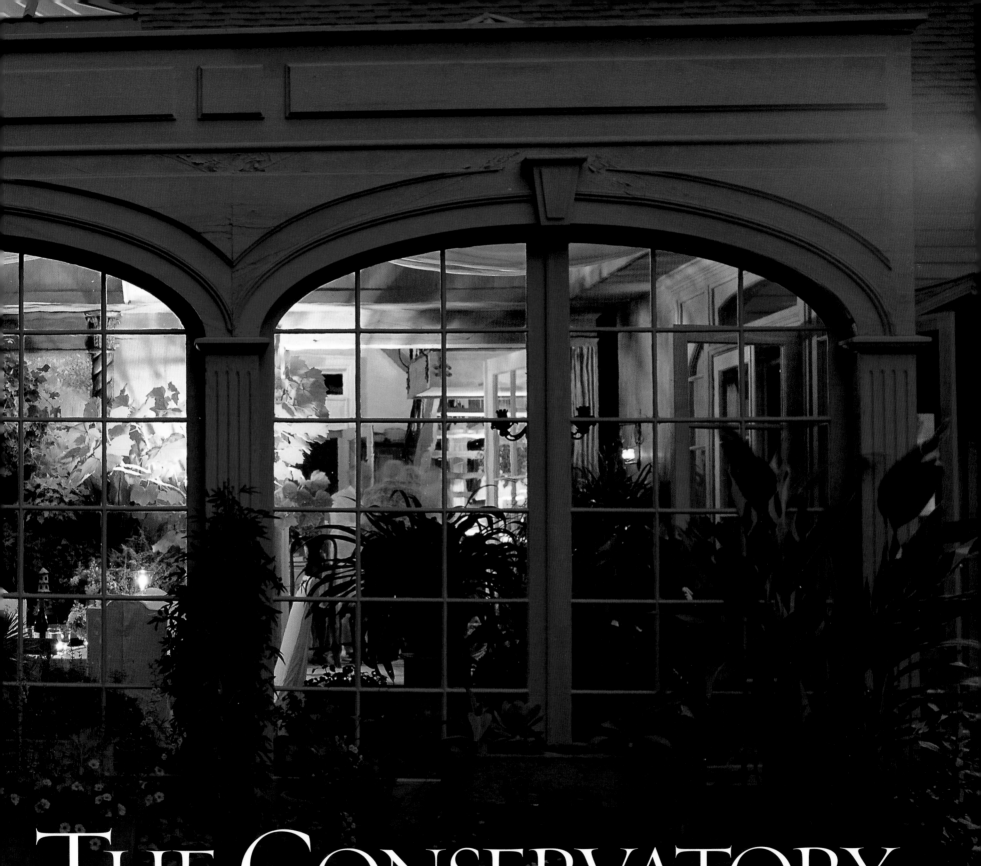

THE CONSERVATORY

THE CONSERVATORY

One day I was driving up Route 7 on my way to the grocery store when I suddenly slammed on the brakes and did a quick U-turn. There, leaning against the side of an antiques shop, were three of the most beautiful arched windows I had ever seen. I went inside and asked the dealer about them. They were old conservatory windows from a Hudson River house that had recently been torn down, and dated from about 1840, just the same period as Manor House. We went out to measure them, and together they were about 32 feet long. I asked the dealer to hold the windows, went and got my groceries, then rushed home. Years ago, I had made a little greenhouse to store plants for the winter and tacked it onto the barn. I went out to measure it—exactly 32 feet long.

It wasn't hard to rip off the greenhouse and make a new room with the conservatory windows. All we had to do was have two more made to match, for the sides. We added skylights to the roof, so the whole place would be filled with light. We paved the room with antique French terra cotta tiles and put the heating system under the floor, which is wonderful for the plants. It keeps their feet warm. A huge stone table stands in the center of the room and can seat twelve for dinner easily.

Of all the spaces in my house or on my property, this is by far my favorite. It's a pocket of summer in winter, when it's filled with camellia, fig, magnolia, and lemon trees. We have night-blooming jasmine climbing up the wall. There are pots of fern and narcissus and other flowering bulbs. You can't imagine how heavenly this room smells.

In summer, most of the trees go outside, the ferns move up to the pool house and more flowering plants take their place. When we sit down for dinner, we'll throw open the doors and the skylights and let the breeze blow through. As the sky darkens, we light the candles. I deliberately kept electric lights out of this room (except for two subtle spotlights that filter up through the leaves). I think the magic of this space has a lot to do with candlelight.

We dine here all through the summer and late into the fall. We'll even be eating out here in December, when snow blankets the ground. After dessert, a few people may move back into the barn to sit by the fire, but there's always a group that wants to stay in this room and keep the conversation going.

OPPOSITE: *The idea of building a conservatory started when I spotted three graceful arched windows propped against the wall of an antiques shop. Now they look out onto the parterre garden, rimmed with brick paths.*

ABOVE: *An antique Belgian linen tablecloth with heavy Brussels lace is my favorite for dinner in the conservatory.* OPPOSITE: *I'll usually have dozens of votives on the table and in brackets around the room. The flickering lights dance across the stone surface and are reflected in the glass as darkness falls.*

Even more important than the food is the atmosphere you

create—that's what people are really going to remember

Above: *With so many potted plants close by, finding a centerpiece for lunch is a snap.* Opposite: *The antique French stone table can seat eighteen, if I add plywood extensions and cover them with cloth. The Italian oak chairs are slipcovered in cotton duck for easy laundering. Simple swathes of cotton duck suspended on a wire track soften the sun pouring through the skylights.*

When grouping plants, it's always important to think
about the texture and size of the leaves. Here, I mixed
very large elephant ear plants with more slender-leafed
specimens like yellow clivia and canna stuttgart.
OPPOSITE: An old stone-topped console table from
France is perfect for plants, since I don't have to worry
about water marring the finish. A candle, a terra
cotta dove, and a tole pagoda are tucked in amidst the
exuberant ferns, ivies, stephanotis, and topiaries.

I don't know many people who can resist John's desserts. Sometimes when we're giving a large dinner party, he will whip up several equally tempting options. One of his specialties is meringues, which can be made conveniently ahead of time and are delicious with ice cream and chocolate sauce. Or you could be more of a purist and simply reach for the fresh fruit, which might be as simple as a plate of sliced oranges or a bowl of ripe strawberries. Add cookies or brownies and you're sure to satisfy everyone. The point is to offer a choice—something sweet and sinful like peach crisp with something lighter like poached pears. Our guests usually want some of each.

Meringue
Makes 24 meringue cookies

4 egg whites, at room temperature
1 cup granulated white sugar
1/2 teaspoon pure vanilla extract
Grated rind of 1/2 lemon

Preheat oven to 225°F. Line a sheet pan with parchment paper. In an electric mixer bowl, beat egg whites on medium/low until frothy. Continue beating while adding sugar in a slow, steady stream. Add lemon rind and vanilla. Turn speed to high and beat for 5 minutes, until the mixture has tripled in volume and has become quite stiff, dense, and glossy.

Drop spoonfuls of meringue on the sheet pan and bake for 1 hour and 10 minutes. The meringue cookies should be baked until they are dry and crisp all the way through. Cool the cookies and serve.

NOTE: The meringue cookies can be stored in an airtight container and will last up to a month.

Peach Crisp
Serves 4 to 6

For the batter:
3/4 stick (4 tablespoons) unsalted butter, cut into bits
2 teaspoons baking powder
1 1/2 cup all-purpose flour
1/2 teaspoon salt
3/4 cup milk
1/2 teaspoon ground cinnamon

2 cups peaches, peeled and sliced
1 cup granulated white sugar

Preheat the oven to 350°F. Place butter in the center of an 8- by 10-inch oval baking dish. Set the dish in the warm oven until the butter has melted. Remove the dish from the oven.

In a medium bowl, combine all other batter ingredients until just mixed together. Spoon batter into the baking dish over the melted butter. Mix the sliced peaches with sugar, and fold them into the batter.

Bake for one hour, until the top is browned and crisp. Serve warm or at room temperature.

NOTE: Other fruits such as rhubarb, fresh blackberries, fresh strawberries, and fresh blueberries (or a combination thereof) can be substituted for the peaches.

Poached Pears
Serves 8

1 cup granulated white sugar
1 quart orange juice
8 firm Bartlett or Anjou pears with stems, peeled
1/2 cup water
1 cup red wine
1/2 cup Grand Marnier liqueur
1 tablespoon pure vanilla extract
Fresh mint leaves (optional)
Fresh whipped cream or vanilla ice cream

Place sugar in a saucepan large enough to hold the pears and set it over low heat. Cook sugar until it is a medium caramel color. Do not stir. Remove pan from heat and very slowly add orange juice. (The mixture will splutter.)

Add pears to pan, and pour water over to barely cover. Simmer over low heat until pears are almost tender, about 10 minutes.

Add wine and liqueur to pan and bring to a boil. Cook until pears are tender, about 5 minutes longer. Remove pears from saucepan and set aside.

Reduce poaching liquid over medium heat to a light syrup, about 15 to 20 minutes. Remove pan from heat and set aside.

When pears and syrup are at room temperature, place pears in a glass serving bowl. Add vanilla to syrup and pour sauce around them. Garnish each pear with mint leaves if desired and serve with whipped cream or vanilla ice cream and cookies of one's choice. Thin French tuiles or ginger cookies would go well with this dish.

INDOOR PLANTS

I have such fun growing plants in pots. From the huge-leafed philodendron that grows happily in the sunny kitchen window to the brightly colored geraniums crowding a tabletop, indoor plants give instant life to the house. When I bring a special plant inside and tuck it into a beautiful cachepot on the corner of a desk or a table, it adds a breath of fresh air to the room.

If ever I were forced to give up the garden, I would always keep one area where I could still grow plants in containers. Half the pleasure for me is continuously moving them around—setting a small, exquisite auricula on a bathroom sink for a guest to enjoy—or arranging various pots of succulents in the center of the dining table in the conservatory. Mixing large ferns with blooming amaryllis makes a lovely still life.

We always order lots of bulbs and force them during the winter months so we can enjoy flowers off-season. The house is even lovelier, filled with the scents of paper whites and hyacinths. When the long wooden boxes of scilla come in from the greenhouse to decorate the center of a luncheon table, I know it is Christmastime.

Larger plants, such as orange trees, infuse the house with the most heavenly aroma in winter and then can be moved outside in summer to bear fruit. Planting and moving pots is one of my favorite things to do.

Favorite Plants

- Amaryllis
- Coleus standards
- Ferns
- Geraniums
- Grape hyacinth
- Iris
- Jasmine
- Orange trees
- Paper white narcissus
- Primula auricula
- Stephanotis
- Succulents

THE

PARTERRE GARDEN

THE PARTERRE GARDEN

As a gardener, I am totally self-taught. But, like any other subject, if you become passionate about it, you read books, go to lectures, and cull tips from other gardeners. I've learned that, just as in interior design, you have to create the floor plan first—which is a little harder to do when you have no floor, just the whole outdoors.

The parterre garden, on the west side of the barn, started out as a vegetable garden with a rather ambitious plan. It was inspired by Rosemary Verey's kitchen garden, which in turn was modeled after the classic French potager. Instead of planting their vegetables in long, straight rows, like the Americans, the French plant them in ornamental patterns—or parterres—that form circles and squares. It's much more fanciful and decorative. But as John and I transformed the barn into a living space, this garden became more formal as well and the working vegetables went elsewhere. But I kept the basic plan.

The garden is bordered by a very simple board fence, which I have allowed to weather to a warm gray. I never painted the fence because I wanted it to disappear into the landscape as if it had always been there. Inside, I laid out a grid of four beds, two large and two small, rimmed by paths made of old, reclaimed brick. The beds are divided by boxwood that forms its own crisscross pattern. Each year, we plant these diamond-shaped areas with a new color scheme. One year, it will be all purple and white—purple salvia, white petunias, ageratum, purple kale (I still use some vegetables, just for their marvelous shapes). The next year we might switch to orange and red—orange coleus, nasturtiums, red salvia, red snapdragons.

Every winter, we lay it all out on paper and decide what is going to go where. For spring, we plant bulbs in our colors. After they've bloomed, they are removed and then the annuals go in. There are several structural elements that reinforce the sense of enclosure and lift your eye to a higher plane. At the north end of

OPPOSITE: *I took my inspiration from early herb gardens when I laid out my parterres. Two dwarf Korean lilacs, with huge ball-shaped heads, are planted in the center of the two larger beds and add an element of height as counterpoint to the flowers. Since this is the view we see from the conservatory, I had to think about how the garden would look all year round. That's when I added the hornbeam hedge, which retains its leaves in winter and looks beautiful laden with snow.*

the garden is a hornbeam hedge that has now grown to a height of about 12 feet, and we added a rusticated pergola covered in climbing roses. Right in the middle of the garden, where the paths cross, is a double metal archway. We always plant this with different vines. Sometimes we try something a little too esoteric that can barely make it up the arch and by the third week of July, I'm fuming, "I hate this vine!"

In the center of each of the two larger beds are two dwarf Korean lilac trees that now measure over six feet. It's always so important to have things that are tall, as well as small. Two large Italian oil jars stand in the middle of the other beds. I love large-scale pots and containers, and often use them as ornaments.

Gardening is all about cultivating the senses—the palette of colors, the scent of the flowers, planting for songbirds. It's the closest I can come to creating peace and solitude. I don't think there's anything more joyous than getting up at 6:00 AM with the birds and going out to look at the garden in the softness of the early morning air, with the dogs running about.

Not that we gardeners are ever satisfied. Visitors may ooh and ah and compliment us on our work, but don't be surprised to hear that perennial response: "Oh, you should have been here last week."

RIGHT: *A double metal archway in the center of the garden marks the point where the two brick paths cross. Every year we plant it with something green and entwining, like a clinging gourd or an ornamental pea vine. The beds are delineated with Victorian rope edging tiles. Handmade Italian terra rosa pots hold tall stalks of heliotrope, which perfumes the breeze with its intoxicating scent.*

Garden geometry and structure is more visible in

spring, before the plants erupt into extravagant bloom

ABOVE: *We made this rustic pergola out of locust saplings, cut down when we cleared another part of the property. The basketweave garden seat doubles as a pedestal, because some plants look better lifted up to eye level. I use a lot of pots and containers because I think they add so much to every nook and cranny of a garden.* OPPOSITE: *The double metal archway is now almost invisible under the flourishing ornamental vine.*

A great garden begins with a strong plan, and

then you can start dreaming about the plants

It takes time
and a lot of
experimentation
to learn which
plants are going
to thrive under
your particular
conditions. Once
you know, you
can start putting
them together
in unusual
combinations

LEFT: *The snake-like shoots of chenopodium undulate around a large Tuscan oil jar in the center of one of the flowerbeds. This year, we chose strong, hot colors and planted bright orange marigolds and verbena "Homestead purple," a great ground cover that blooms all summer long.*

Every property needs what I call the service area—the behind-the-scenes precinct where the nitty-gritty work gets done. Ours begins with the utility barn. When we turned the old barn into living space, we still had to find somewhere to store all those storm windows and skis, not to mention the tractor. So we built a new utility barn, modeled after a 19th-century carriage house in town.

Next to it is the vegetable garden, where John spends half of every weekend. We grow the vegetables we want to eat. As one crop ripens, we pick it and enjoy it. Then we take that row out and plant another crop. It's not like a flower garden; it's a whole different philosophy: Everything in this garden is going to be consumed. Oddly enough, the perennial borders take less effort once they're established. But we have to be in this garden every day, weeding and staking and picking tomatoes, beans, and beets.

You can't imagine what it's like to eat potatoes when they're freshly pulled from the ground. Truman Capote once famously remarked that the difference between himself and rich people was the size of their vegetables. It's true. A carrot is sweeter when it's smaller. A tiny potato has a texture like cream. Bite into a vine-ripened tomato and you're tempted to eat it like an apple. Of course it's not practical. I hate to think what my salads must cost me. But there is such delight in knowing that I planted that seed, watched it turn into a head of lettuce, and then ate it.

THE SERVICE AREA

Every large garden
needs a working
area, out of public
view, where
seedlings can be
started and plants
that require a bit
of help can be
nursed along. A
lot of labor takes
place behind the
scenes before the
play can go on

LEFT: *Orchids rest on tiered shelves by the greenhouse wall, left to go dormant in summer until they bloom again and brighten the dark winter days. A metal table surrounded by vintage French spring- metal chairs is set in the shade of an old walnut tree—the perfect spot for a quick lunch during a busy working day.*

THE CUTTING &
VEGETABLE GARDEN

The vegetable garden shares space with the cutting garden, and every year we face the same territorial imperative. John needs lots of vegetables for his cooking and I need lots of flowers for the house. Supposedly, we decide how much of the plot goes to flowers and how much to vegetables by a barter system. In reality, I tell Eric Ruquist, our gardener, one thing and John tells him something else. ("She invariably wins," says John.)

I plant flowers in the colors I need for the house. The tulips bloom first—apricot for the living room, dark red and black for the barn, white for the dining room. I'll cut branches of lilac, quince or apple blossom to give me the scale I need for a big arrangement in the hallway or the barn. Every year I plant a 30-foot-long row of peonies, single and double, in all different shades from white to deep pink to dark red. I just love peonies, and I can't wait till they bloom in June.

At the height of summer, there are snapdragons and zinnias, sunflowers and bells of Ireland. I'll plant rows of coleus, which has such a nice leaf color, and larkspur, and tons of dahlias. I adore dahlias, in any variation or theme. Now, some people dismiss gladiolas as funereal but I happen to love big, tall stalks of gladiola mixed into an arrangement. They add an interesting spike when other flowers are more rounded. Another unexpected combination that works well is gladiolas and sunflowers. I saw it first on a hall table in France, and thought, "Gosh, I have never seen gladiolas look so good in my life."

In one corner, I've planted herbs. I use wattle fencing and make little patterns with the parsley, sage, rosemary, and thyme. This garden is a wonderful organic tapestry of texture and color, with a backdrop of rich soil.

OPPOSITE: *A row of dark leafy kale, which John likes to use in soup, becomes a blue-green background for ageratum "red top"—perfect for bouquets since it lasts a long time after it is cut. The bed progresses from small, medium, to large plants, with the top-heavy tomatoes tied to wooden ladders for support.*

John and I always have a tug of war over the kitchen garden

The early 19th-century picket fence around the cutting garden was rescued from demolition in Maine and wound up at the Farmington antiques fair, where we bought it. At the rear of the garden is the greenhouse. OPPOSITE: The new utility barn, detailed with board and batten, sits behind rows of snapdragons, dahlias, and zucchini.

how much for vegetables and how much for flowers

I divided this large garden into three rectangles and installed gravel paths so I could walk between the beds. This makes for much easier maintenance and allows closer access to the flowers and vegetables. A French metal urn shows off our *Beschorneria Yuccoides*, otherwise known as Mexican lily, underplanted with helichrysum.

I think you should only plant flowers that you love. I choose colors that will work with my rooms, so I can always go into the garden and come out with a bouquet. Dahlias are one of our favorite flowers, and I love the purplish-red petals of salpiglossis, which look as if they were painted with watercolors. The tall vine is Dolichos Lablab "Ruby Moon", also known as hyacinth bean.

DISCOVERING EXOTIC PLANTS

Almost all gardeners at some point become fascinated with exotic plants. We get bored seeing the same things over and over and are always looking for the unusual. Of course, the plant that intrigues me most is often exactly the one that won't grow in my climate zone—which is another justification for building a greenhouse. Some exotic plants can survive outside in warmer climates. Luckily, more and more nurseries are broadening their scope and searching out plants that can be grown as annuals, if you don't have a place to winter them over.

Most of my tender exotics begin their life indoors in pots, and move outside once the weather gets warmer. I first fell in love with plumbago when I saw it growing in the garden of the Villa Gambaria, in the hills of Fiesole outside Florence. Now, in Connecticut, four pots of these sky blue flowers come outdoors each spring and are placed on the stone wall of the sunken garden. The magnolia grandiflora trees that live in the corners of the conservatory remind me of Virginia. My favorite hydrangea, "Madame Emile Mouillere," flourishes in large pots at the entrance to the barn. I'll often use cannas at the back of a border for a vibrant shot of color.

What I like most about exotic plants is their scale—huge bold leaves that look wonderful either in pots or in a perennial border, where great scale is an asset. The gigantic leaves of a banana plant look regal, silhouetted against the old picket fence in the kitchen garden. Exotic plants can reinvigorate even the dullest spot and add a touch of magic to any setting.

Favorite Plants

- Alocasia
- Banana
- Brugmansia
- Camellia
- Colocasia
- Crinum
- Cyperus papyrus

- Duranta
- Eucomis
- Hedychium "Ginger Lily"
- Haemanthus multiflorus
- Hydrangea

- "Madame Emile Mouillere"
- Iochroma cyaneum
- Magnolia grandiflora
- Orange and Lime
- Plumbago
- Prostanthera

THE GREENHOUSE

At the far end of the cutting garden stands the greenhouse. For me, it is the soul of the place. I can always tell who the real gardeners are because they want to see my greenhouse. And I'm exactly the same way. When I visit a famous garden like Vita Sackville-West's Sissinghurst or Christopher Lloyd's Great Dixter, I can't wait to get to the back part of the garden, where you see the hoses and the wheelbarrows and all the things that go into making this perfection.

It all starts in the greenhouse. Whenever I buy a new plant from the nursery, I bring it here first. This is my holding tank, where everything waits while I decide where I'm going to put it. I think of this as the intellectual side of the garden—a place to try something new, to get my hands dirty while I experiment. I'll start seedlings, not sure if they're going to grow. Some don't. But you'll never have an interesting garden if you don't take risks.

When you have a garden that people come to look at all the time, you naturally want it to be perfect. You feel compelled to have everything in garden-show shape every day. But plants aren't like that. We all have our moments, and that's why I have the plant hospital. This is where my invalids go to recover. It's like taking care of a sick child, and just as challenging. Sometimes I have to prescribe isolation, or at least seclusion, until they perk up.

I can't imagine not having a greenhouse. It allows me to garden twelve months a year. Otherwise I would be housebound from November to May. There is nothing better on a cold day than to be up in the greenhouse, deadheading flowers so they'll bloom again, feeding and watering, repotting plants that have grown too big for their containers. It's a very maternal thing to do, and very important for the garden.

Having a greenhouse allows me to bring the more fragile plants inside to winter over. I can force bulbs and fill the house with blossoms even in December. It may be snowing outside, but it's always warm in the greenhouse. It smells of jasmine and orange blossom and good, clean earth.

OPPOSITE: *Eric Ruquist, the head gardener, is in the greenhouse making labels for newly potted plants. As they grow bigger, the plants move to the garden or the conservatory, but many come back to the greenhouse for the cold months. I love acidanthera (way in the back) for its tall thin leaves and its pure white flower that has a delicious scent.*

THE CHICKEN PAVILION

John is a bird lover, and beloved by birds in turn. He has one peacock who will sit on his shoulder and wrap her neck around him, or tuck her head under his arm. You'd swear he was St. Francis of Assisi, the way birds follow him around. He used to have a huge chicken coop at his house in New Jersey, and I built this chicken house as a birthday present for him.

It's modeled after one I saw in England, and consists of two square pavilions connected by an octagonal wire aviary. The chicken wire extends over the top of the cage and deep into the ground, otherwise foxes and rodents could get in and kill the birds. White fantail pigeons live in one pavilion and chickens in the other, and they meet in the middle.

Don't think for a moment that there is anything practical about this arrangement. We are not raising these chickens for food. The only thing we get is wonderful fresh eggs. Not a morsel of their meat has ever crossed our lips. In fact, I call this John's retirement home for chickens. They all tend to live to a very old age here, and finally drop dead from senility—or egotism. John tends to pick ornamental breeds that can be too pretty for their own good. The Polish chicken has a ridiculous topknot and a snooty glare that reminds me of an old Palm Beach matron in her most elegant hat. The Silver Sebrights have wonderful white feathers edged in black. Then there are excellent layers, like the Rhode Island Reds. If you just sit for half an hour and watch them all strutting around and preening for each other, I guarantee that you'll be enthralled, too.

If we're working in the garden nearby, we often let them out to range freely—to Eric's dismay, since they head straight for the vegetables and start digging—who says chickens aren't smart? Well, they may not be the most intelligent animals around, but they are certainly the most amusing.

OPPOSITE: *The aviary adds a fanciful touch of Chinoiserie to the Connecticut countryside and keeps the birds safe from predators (not to mention dogs, who think that nothing is more fun than chasing chickens). Matching pavilions on each side give all our feathered friends a cozy place to sleep.*

ABOVE: *The fantail pigeons like to roost on poles at the top of the tower-like pavilion. Tiny arched holes, just big enough for a bird, are cut high into the walls so the pigeons can fly in and out as they please.*
OPPOSITE: *John's beloved peacock poses in front of a round window.*

THE POOL HOUSE

THE POOL HOUSE

About three years ago, John announced, "What we really need around here is a swimming pool." I said, "There's no place to put a pool." But of course John already had that figured out. He had picked out a sunny spot up on the hill just beyond the orchard. That's about as far as we got, until we were standing in a stone-cutter's lot in the south of France. John was poking around, looking for items for our garden shop, Treillage, when I suddenly heard him shout, "I've found the swimming pool!" I came over to his side, and stared down at these huge blocks of limestone, suitable for a Parisian *bassin*. John thought they would make the perfect coping for our pool, so that was that.

Let me just say I don't advise shipping a warm French stone to cold Connecticut. It's not as hardy as we would like. But it does look beautiful.

Once we had a pool, we needed a pool house. (A fatal progression with which we're all too familiar—one project begets another.) Clearly, the pool was too far away to rely on the main house. So now we were faced with the delightful question—what should we build? I had no interest in the typical white-latticed pool house. While we were in France, I had picked up a book on 18th-century garden follies and one picture caught my eye. It showed a brick building with a porch, and the porch columns were made out of tree trunks. That was the genesis of the idea, and then it grew from there. The village in Connecticut where we live is full of wonderful Greek Revival architecture. Why not erect our own little Greek temple, and make it out of tree trunks?

I talked to a friend who is an architect and asked him to give me the mathematical formula for a classic Greek temple—what were the proportions of height, width and depth? Then I took these figures and the book and went to see our local carpenter, Gerald McMahon. I sketched out a design on a napkin and he took it from there and did an amazing job. It's not easy to find 10 trees that could work as columns with straight trunks of about the same height and width. But Gerald did. He located an old

OPPOSITE: *The idea for the rusticated temple pool house came from a book I found on 18th-century garden follies, and it seemed appropriate since our town is famous for Greek Revival architecture. One side of the pool is lined with underwater steps—the perfect place to cool off on a hot summer day. John and I will often get in with the dogs and read the paper. We shipped the eight-foot-wide bamboo umbrellas home from India.*

estate where a grove of white oaks was about to be cut down for redevelopment. He walked through and measured every tree and marked the ones he wanted. Then he had to wrap all ten trunks in blankets, so that the bark wouldn't be rubbed off when they were chained together for transport.

The earliest Greek temples were made of wood, but I doubt that they came equipped with a handcarved limestone fireplace and a kitchen. We'll often go up just before lunch, have a swim, and then eat in the shade of the pavilion. In fall, with the fire lit, it's a lovely spot for drinks and dinner.

I'll never forget one Saturday when I was hosting the annual Trade Secrets benefit flower show. Even though it was May 18th, it started to snow. Everybody huddled around the fire in the pool house to warm up and then went out and bought more plants.

We sited the building on the crest of the hill, for the view.

Just beyond is the forest, and I wanted the pavilion to look natural, as if the trees had simply come out of the woods to make this building. Every property has a sense of place, and if you think about how a building could express that before you start the design and construction process, you'll often get something a lot more interesting. You can see our temple from a country road, and sometimes people will stop their cars and stare. Once, I was working nearby in the garden when a young couple got out of their car and asked if it was a historic monument. I couldn't resist replying, "Yes, and it was built by a crazy lady who lived here." But I don't really think I'm crazy, just obsessed.

ABOVE: *In such a natural place, I wanted everything to feel organic. Unglazed pots are gathered around a big Mexican terra cotta apple on the bamboo coffee table.*
OPPOSITE: *The expansive open-air room is furnished with rattan chairs and wooden tables. An elaborately carved circular ceiling panel from Indonesia hangs over the French limestone mantel, just behind a carved wooden deer from India.*

OPPOSITE: *A frieze of split logs runs along the top of the pool house. In a whimsical touch, I filled the pediment with pinecones.* ABOVE: *The atmospheric mural on the changing room walls was painted by Clifton Jaeger on crackled canvas and evokes the feeling of an ancient tapestry. The wainscoting is made from old, weathered boards.*

ABOVE: *Feathery ferns in large terra cotta pots bring the forest inside.* OPPOSITE: *When I sit under the soaring timbered roof of the pool pavilion and see bark still clinging to the columns, I feel as if I've stumbled onto Arcadia. The 19th-century French farm table, surrounded with 1920s Belgian rattan chairs, is the scene of many summer lunches.*

I wanted the building to feel as if the trees had just waltzed

out of the woodland and formed a Greek temple

I often treat lunches or suppers at the pool house more like a picnic. When you're sitting in this wide-open room, ruffled by the breeze, you almost feel as if you're still out-doors. We usually prepare the food in the main house in the morning and then bring it up in baskets (this is where our "Gator," a lit-tle John Deere tractor, comes in handy). The pool house kitchen is stocked with all the necessary drinks, dishes, glasses, flatware, and linens (we'll use tin plates and plastic glasses for the children)—so all we need is the food. I'll often make a green salad from whatever is ready in the garden—lettuces, spinach, or arugula. Dessert is usually cookies, brownies, and fresh fruit—especially watermelon on a hot summer day.

Mother-in-Law Coleslaw
Serves 8

1 large white cabbage, tough outer
　　leaves discarded
1 cup Hellmann's mayonnaise
2 tablespoons celery seed
1 teaspoon salt, or to taste
1 teaspoon freshly ground white pepper

Chop cabbage into small pieces (not strips), about $1/2$ to $1/4$ inches. Some pieces should be larger for a crunchy texture. In a large bowl, combine mayonnaise, celery seed, salt, and pepper. Add the cabbage and toss to coat. Cover with plastic wrap and refrigerate for at least 2 hours, tossing occasionally. Serve cold.

Cold Poached Chicken Breasts
Serves 8

8 boneless chicken breasts, skinless
1 1/2 cups water
1/2 cup chicken stock
1 cup Hellmann's mayonnaise
1 1/2 tablespoons curry powder
1 tablespoon freshly squeezed lemon juice
1 bunch Italian parsley or chives,
　　finely chopped

Poach chicken breasts slowly in water and chicken stock until tender, about 15 to 20 minutes. Remove the chicken from poach-ing liquid, cover with plastic wrap, and place in the refrigerator until ready to serve. In the meantime, combine the may-onnaise with the curry powder and lemon juice. When ready to serve, place the chick-en on a large platter. Spread the curried mayonnaise over the top of each breast and dress the platter with parsley or chives.

Tuna and Green Bean Salad
Serves 6

FOR THE VINAIGRETTE
Makes 1/2 cup

2 tablespoons balsamic vinegar
1/4 teaspoon fine sea salt
1/2 cup olive oil
Freshly ground pepper to taste

FOR THE SALAD
1 pound green beans, trimmed
2 hard-boiled eggs
1/2 head Iceberg lettuce, leaves separated,
　　washed, and patted dry
1 head Romaine lettuce, leaves separated,
　　washed, and patted dry
2 (6-ounce) cans solid white chunk tuna
　　packed in water, drained and divided

In a small bowl combine the vinegar and salt, and stir until the salt dissolves. Add the olive oil slowly, whisking until emulsified, then the pepper. Set aside.

In a saucepan, parboil green beans, about 3 minutes, until crisp-tender. Set aside. Chop hard-boiled eggs and set aside. Chop lettuce leaves and place in a large salad bowl. Add green beans, tuna, and eggs to salad bowl and toss to mix thoroughly. Whisk the vinai-grette again, and drizzle over the salad.

Tomato Aspic
Serves 8

1 quart V-8 juice
1/2 cup cold water
2 tablespoons gelatin
1 bunch celery, chopped
One 4-ounce jar Spanish green olives stuffed
　　with pimentos, drained and chopped
1 tablespoon finely-grated onion

Heat V-8 juice in a saucepan to boiling point and set aside. Pour water in a small saucepan and sprinkle in the powdered gelatin. Let gelatin dissolve for at least 10 minutes. Add gelatin to heated V-8 juice and stir until the liquid is clear. Let mixture cool completely and then add celery, olives, and onion.

Pour tomato-gelatin mixture into a large ring mold and cover loosely with plastic wrap. Place mold in the refrigerator and let it set overnight. When you are ready to serve, remove the mold from the refrigera-tor and dip it quickly in a pan of very hot tap water. Turn the mold over on a serving plate and tap sharply, releasing the aspic. Serve with a chicken or shrimp salad mounded in the center.

THE WOODLAND

GARDEN

T

The problem with being a gardener is that as soon as you get one garden finished, you start looking over the fence. For a number of years, I was content to cultivate my various plots. I would walk down the path from the house and open the gate to the parterre garden, stepping into the dappled light under an arbor brimming with clematis and honeysuckle. Then one day I looked up and realized if I put a gate on the opposite side of the fence I could keep going—just because it was there.

That's why it's dangerous for someone like me to own 12 acres. I'm tempted by all the possibilities, instead of being satisfied with what I've already done. The parterre garden may be flourishing—after years of devoted work—but my eye is already straying. From a design standpoint, I'm bored. As soon as one creation is up and running, I get itchy to create again. It's a bit like giving birth to a child—three years later you're ready to have another one.

So I set down my gloves and clippers and went over to walk that part of the property. If you want to make a successful garden, you have to let the land tell you what to do. I was facing a hillside covered with woods, overgrown and wild, and I wandered all over until I found a way to navigate it comfortably. I decided I needed some stone steps in the slope to mark the beginning of my path. Then I planted four soaring arborvitae, clipped to remind me of cypress—this is what I call my Italian moment. They frame a great stone urn at the top of the steps, which is planted with an exuberant bouquet every summer.

Up at the top of the hill, near a 200-year-old maple, the land formed a natural bowl. This had become the repository for all sorts of rusted tractor parts over the years. But I looked at that glorious tree and the ancient rock formations and that dip in the ground and thought, this would make a wonderful pond. Now, there happens to be no water on my property. So I did some research and found a man who could come and create a pond out of nothing and make it look utterly natural. He lugged some boulders around and rigged up a waterfall that seems to spill spontaneously out of the rocks—and then the water recirculates through the pond. It's such a delight to walk through the trees and follow the sound of rushing water.

I planted irises and primula all around the edge of the pond. Primula is such an old-fashioned flower. You never see it cut; it only works as a plant. Part of its charm is that it has never been civilized. I always feel happy to spot that bright green leaf with its shocking pink or white blossoms. In spring, it carpets the ground.

Of course, it took years to get it to look like that. There is nothing that brings you to your knees more quickly than trying to do a natural garden. It's much trickier than simply planting a small, contained plot, where you can water and fertilize at will. In a woodland garden, you are not in control. You have to try various plants, and hope they will like the conditions and do well. If I want to carpet an area with primula, I'll buy maybe 500 plugs that cost 50 cents apiece and watch how they do for a few years. Ideally, they will go native and spread. But it doesn't happen overnight. In fact, they might die out and you'll have to start all over again, with something else.

Yet some plants love the shade and the inhospitable soil, and when I find those, I buy more of them. I planted an array of ferns, as well as tipularias, epimediums, and viburnum. In spring, this is the earliest garden to bloom because I've salted

OPPOSITE: *Tall arborvitae trees line the steps that lead to the woodland garden and frame a view of a 19th-century English urn—a focal point meant to lure you further into the garden. Every year we fill it with a different combination of plants, such as canna Australia, lotus berthelotii, coleus, and datura. The arrangement has to be very large in scale so it will read from afar.*

the hills with thousands of bulbs. Even before the leaves on the trees are out, the ground is ablaze with masses of daffodils, fritillarias, scillas, and crocuses.

Under that majestic maple, I placed a table, a bench, and two chairs, where I can sit with a friend over a pitcher of iced tea. Or I might make some deviled eggs and pimento cheese sandwiches, pack them into a basket and spread out a picnic on the grass. In the heat of summer, this is the coolest place on the property. Occasionally a carp breaks the glassy surface of the pond, which registers the movement of each passing cloud. The sky is doubled.

I was inspired by what was already there when I made this garden, and it has evolved over time. Today, some people buy a property, draw up a site plan, and do everything at once. I didn't. I couldn't afford to. Instead, each garden appeared as I gradually got to know the land and began to explore another area of the site. I started with the sunken garden because I wanted something to look at from the house. Then, as we took over the barn and spent more and more time in the conservatory, new gardens arrived to complement those buildings. Sometimes I think it's better this way, that the gardens really do fit the property, but I'll admit there's some quirkiness. I didn't anticipate the expansion of the parterre garden and sometimes things don't line up as well as they should, but I refuse to let it bother me.

Gardening for me is not merely an aesthetic experience—it's spiritual. It's always astounding to me how a tiny little seed grows into this amazing plant. It's also humbling. How could I ever create something as beautiful as that? Once I saw John pick up a stumpy branch at the nursery and asked, "Why are you buying that teeny tree?" He answered, "Don't you understand? The trees on the property are already 200 years old. If someone is still living here in 100 years, they're going to need another tree, and we should plant it."

Can you imagine planting an oak? I'm too impatient to wait 50 years for anything. To start something you'll never enjoy in your lifetime is an unselfish act. I'm in awe of anyone who can plant a seed for a tree. I'm not there yet, but I'm working on it.

OPPOSITE: *The pond we made out of a hole in the ground, complete with a little waterfall bubbling out of the rocks, looks as if it has been here forever. It's a wonderful spot for an impromptu picnic. We'll spread a patchwork quilt over the ground and lean back against the portable chairs, drinking iced tea with our sandwiches.*

OPPOSITE: *This woodland bower is furnished with a 19th-century French cast-cement table and chairs, meant to look as if they were made from branches and twigs.* ABOVE: *Garden ornaments, like this statue of the goddess Atlanta, are very useful because they draw your attention to things you might otherwise miss—like the stand of cimicifuga with its arching stems waving in the breeze around her.*

When we're having a picnic under the apple trees,

I like to spread the straw rugs we found in Morocco over the long grass of the meadow, and scatter a few cushions around for a soft perch on a lazy afternoon. Lightweight folding chairs surround a folding table, draped with an Indian bedspread. I have a passion for old picnic baskets— although this one is more like a picnic suitcase—packed with plates and cups and Bakelite-handled flatware.

I feel as if I'm in an Impressionist painting

EATING OUTDOORS

For some reason I adore eating outdoors in all sorts of different spots on the property. I think it goes back to the fun I had as a child, preparing for tailgate picnics with my parents at various horse events. I loved making little sandwiches and deviled eggs and packing everything in baskets. It really is a wonderful way to entertain. Everyone can share in the preparation and there is no laborious clean-up when the meal is over. It also gets you out to enjoy a special spot—sitting in the garden, by a pond, or under a shady tree in an orchard, intoxicated by the smell of apple blossoms.

A picnic can be put together simply with a delicious loaf of bread, a hunk of cheese, the best salami or pastrami, fresh fruit, and cookies. Just add a bottle of wine or a thermos of iced tea. It's the perfect kind of summer entertaining and great fun for everybody, especially children and dogs.

Picnic Sandwiches

FOR ALL SANDWICH RECIPES:
1 loaf thin-sliced white or whole wheat bread
Each recipe makes enough filling for approximately 30 half sandwiches.

TO ASSEMBLE:
Spread half the bread slices with the filling and cover with a slice of fish or meat, if recipe so indicates. Place the other piece of bread on top. Cut each sandwich in half on the diagonal.

Smoked Salmon Spread

1/4 cup sour cream
1/2 cup cream cheese
2 tablespoons finely chopped chives
1 pound Scottish-style smoked salmon, sliced

Put the sour cream and cream cheese in a food processor and blend, or thoroughly mix in a medium bowl. Add the chives. Refrigerate, covered with plastic wrap, for at least an hour. Remove from the refrigerator 30 minutes before assembling sandwiches.

Chicken with Chutney Mayonnaise

1/2 cup Hellmann's mayonnaise
2 tablespoons Major Grey's Chutney, finely chopped
2 poached skinless chicken breasts, finely chopped

In a medium bowl, combine the mayonnaise and chutney. Mix in the chicken. Refrigerate, covered with plastic wrap, for at least an hour. Remove from the refrigerator 30 minutes before assembling sandwiches.

Black Forest Ham with Mustard Mayonnaise

1/2 cup Hellmann's mayonnaise
1 tablespoon brown mustard
1 pound Black Forest ham

In a small bowl, combine mayonnaise and mustard.

Peanut Butter and Honey

Peanut butter
Honey, preferably clover

Spread half the bread slices with peanut butter and the other half with honey.

Egg Salad

2 hard-boiled eggs
1 tablespoon dried mustard powder
Salt and freshly ground black pepper to taste
1/4 to 1/3 cup Hellmann's mayonnaise to taste

Chop the eggs medium-fine and place in a medium bowl. Stir in mustard, salt, pepper, and mayonnaise. Refrigerate, covered with plastic wrap, for at least an hour. Remove from the refrigerator 30 minutes before assembling sandwiches.

Pimento Cheese

1 pound sharp Cheddar cheese, grated
1/3 cup Hellmann's mayonnaise
1/2 teaspoon cayenne pepper
One 4-ounce jar pimentos, drained and finely diced

Put all ingredients in a food processor and blend, or thoroughly mix with a hand mixer in a medium bowl. Refrigerate, covered with plastic wrap, for at least an hour, or overnight. Remove from the refrigerator 30 minutes before assembling sandwiches.

THE GUEST HOUSE

THE GUEST HOUSE

When I first saw Manor House, I immediately noticed the most beautiful specimen of Greek Revival architecture right across the street. The small white clapboard house had four fat Doric columns in front, topped by a graceful pediment. The minute I saw it I thought it would be perfect for my dear friend Alan Campbell, a fabric designer who was passionate about classical architecture.

Unfortunately, it belonged to someone else, an elderly lady named Mrs. Dixon. Soon after I moved in, I rang her bell and introduced myself. I made great friends with Mrs. Dixon and had her over many times for lunch or tea, usually when Alan was visiting as well. This courtship was not an overnight success. In fact, five years went by, until one night I noticed she had left her car's headlights on and walked over to tell her. When she opened the door, she said, "Oh, I've been meaning to talk to you. You have to tell that nice young Mr. Campbell to give me a call." Trying not to look too gleeful, I practically ran home and went straight to the phone to tell Alan.

He bought the lovely house from Mrs. Dixon, and lived there happily for 16 years. I fully expected he would be there forever. Unfortunately, life works in mysterious ways, and Alan died in

2000. The house came into my hands, because I couldn't quite imagine anyone else owning it. Around the time I took possession, my stepmother passed away, and a great many family heirlooms—china, paintings, furniture—came back to me and found a new home here. It was as if several narratives had come full circle. Mr. Brewster, the owner of Manor House, had originally built this house in 1850 for his son, and now it was once again part of the property.

We use it as a guest house, to handle the weekend overflow—and the furniture overflow. At first glance, with those four imposing columns, the house seems very grand, but as soon as you walk in you realize it's really tiny. I've decided that Mr. Brewster was probably a hardworking man who had a dandy for a son—why else would the son have a grander-looking house than his parents? The ground floor is a miniature version of Manor House, with a living room, dining room, library, and a stair hall on the side. Upstairs are two bedrooms.

Though the rooms are small in scale, there is no timidity about the architecture. Period details, like pilasters and moldings, are strong and bold. The house has an elegance far beyond its size, and I had no desire to tamper with its character. But I did make a few strategic modifications. I opened up a door between the library and the living room, because a small room appears much larger if you can look through to another room. I also took down a wall to make a comfortable eat-in kitchen.

I wanted the house to feel very light and open. There are no curtains in the living room because I like to see all the beautiful woodwork. The sofa is a formal American mahogany piece, probably made about the same time as the house, but then I mixed in some Swedish neoclassical furniture and a pair of white-painted Italian chairs that I've had since I first came to New York. The library is still filled with Alan's books, which he left to me. The wicker furniture on the screened porch dates from John's first house in the Hamptons, which he owned more years ago than he would like me to admit. That's why it makes sense to only buy pieces that you truly love. Even if you don't use something for a while, you're always happy to have it back.

I love getting the house ready—putting out the latest *Vanity Fair*, arranging flowers by the bed. In fact, I make sure I've spent a night in each of my guest rooms, so I can see if there is anything missing. I stock the kitchen with cereal, muffins, fruit, and coffee so guests don't have to tiptoe around waiting for John and me to get up, but can simply get breakfast for themselves.

There's a lot of planning involved in being a good hostess, but people also have to know how to be good guests. I keep a basket of maps and brochures on a table in the dining room, so people can preview the local sites and figure out what they might like to do. Some are eager to go off antiquing, others just want to relax by the pool. Then everyone regroups for dinner. It's fun to put everybody to work, helping to pick vegetables and set the table. But if a guest expects to be entertained all day and can't be independent, he probably won't be asked back.

There's something about a rocking chair on a porch that I find very nostalgic. It's absolutely wonderful to come out here early in the morning and sit with a cup of coffee, listening to the birds while the sun warms your face.

ABOVE: *I found this metal sign and presented it to Alan one Christmas. It marks the spot where I always crossed the street to go visit him.* RIGHT: *A gap in the picket fence lines up with the driveway to Manor House, making for easy access back and forth. A large urn at the end of the flagstone path is filled with walking iris.*

This Greek Revival gem is a small house with a very large presence. In deference to the original architectural details, which are all intact, I kept the colors and the furnishings in the main rooms very simple

LEFT: *The morning sun pours through the open front door, sending shafts of light over the needlepoint rug in the entrance hall.* OPPOSITE: *A painted English sofa table stands in front of a tall English Regency mirror. I bought the pair of Italian Directoire chairs for my first New York apartment more than 30 years ago.*

Even when there are no guests, I'll sometimes come here

OPPOSITE: *The 19th-century American mahogany sofa in the living
room is completely uncomfortable but utterly elegant, and belongs to the same
period as the house. A contemporary charcoal drawing hangs over it.*
ABOVE: *I inherited the English mahogany drop-front desk in the library
from my father. I've stocked it with postcards and stationery, but it's
far more likely that a guest will sit down with his laptop and answer e-mails.*

and work on the jigsaw puzzle and think of Alan

Since few dinners are eaten at this dining table, I decided to turn it into command central for guests—stacked with books, brochures about local attractions, maps of the area, and disposable cameras. OPPOSITE: The historic scenic wallpaper by Zuber is a fitting backdrop for some of John's collection of Chinese Export porcelain. He designed the brass hurricane candlesticks, modeled on an 18th-century original.

ABOVE: *Plaid taffeta curtains blend right in with the colors of the Zuber wallpaper—a scenic panorama called Hindoustan— originally printed in France about the time the house was built.* OPPOSITE: *A 1950s gilt mirror hangs over a French Restoration console table laden with more blue-and-white china. The curtain valances were inspired by a Turkish design.*

PREPARING FOR GUESTS

There is nothing worse than being the guest of a host who is working so hard that it is impossible for anyone to have a good time. This only makes people feel uncomfortable and convinced they are imposing. All this is easy to avoid if you plan carefully. John and I want the weekends to be relaxing for everyone, including us.

A good host makes entertaining seem effortless. We try to do as much as possible beforehand, so we are not stuck in the kitchen instead of enjoying the company of our guests. Plan the meals in advance, and make things like soups, pastas, sauces, brownies, and meringues ahead of time. Keep it simple, and give each guest a chore. People like to help set the table or wash the lettuce.

If you have guests who want to play golf, hike, or ski, do some investigating and make arrangements for them. I do not feel that it is my job to entertain my guests all day, but I do provide the information they need to go off on their own. In the evening, we may ask mutual friends to join us for dinner, or invite someone we think they might like to meet. At the end of the weekend, you want guests to feel that they have had a great time and you should all look forward to doing it again.

On the Table
- Books
- DVDs
- The latest magazines
- Maps
- Brochures of local attractions
- Binoculars
- Disposable cameras

In the Closet
- Summer hats
- Winter hats
- Scarves
- Gloves
- Raincoats
- Windbreakers
- Umbrellas
- Boots

In the Kitchen
- Coffee
- Tea
- Milk
- Half-and-half
- Cereal
- Muffins
- Fruit

For the Kids
- Books
- DVDs
- Jigsaw puzzles
- Board games
- Deck of cards
- Jacks
- Jump rope
- Kites
- Art supplies

RIGHT: *The kitchen table consists of an English Directoire painted base with a faux-marble top. The Queen Anne-style chairs are painted a crisp, clean white and upholstered with a simple striped cotton. The 1950s cabinet with glass doors is perfect for displaying china.*

Spending time with friends and family means so much to us and is a wonderful break from our busy lives

ABOVE LEFT: *A small bathroom has a black-and-white theme, with patterned wallpaper, checked curtains, white paint, and black frames all mixed together for a graphic effect.* CENTER: *A painted desk doubles as a dressing table.* OPPOSITE: *John refinished a simple four-poster bed from Crate & Barrel with black lacquer. Above it hangs a vintage fireboard that came with the house.*

WHAT EVERY GUEST ROOM NEEDS

I want these rooms to feel very special. I think of them as a retreat where friends can get away and relax, as if they were on vacation, even though it's only for a short period of time.

Before your guests arrive, open a window to let in some fresh air. At dusk, I'll go up and switch on a lamp so no one has to walk into an unfamiliar room in the dark. Make sure the pillows are puffed up and turn down the sheets—it's a simple gesture that makes anyone feel pampered.

For the Bed

- Comfortable bed with crisply ironed sheets. I like Egyptian cotton percale, with a 400 thread count—more body than satin but still very soft. For a fresh, fragrant touch, add lavender or rose geranium water to the rinse cycle on washday—almost as good as hanging them out on the line to dry in the sun.
- Lots of pillows, including two large 27-inch European squares for reading in bed. I'll put two such squares and four standard pillows on a queen-size bed. Treat yourself and your friends to luxurious down pillows—you can order them straight from the Company Store—but keep one good-

quality Dacron or polyester pillow in the closet for guests with allergies.
- Soft throw over the foot of the bed for naps. Choose cashmere, silk, or one of those wonderfully light cotton voile throws from the Company Store, Garnet Hill, or the Chambers catalogue.
- Fold a duvet over the foot of the bed for chilly nights.

On the Table

- Fresh flowers
- Books, new and old. Try to put something on top that your guest might particularly enjoy.
- Magazines, both current newsweeklies and vintage copies of *Country Life, World of Interiors,* or *Art & Antiques.* Splurge on glossy European magazines and gossipy tabloids.
- Good reading lamps on both sides of the bed. I'll tuck a small tensor lamp in back, in case one partner wants to read while the other sleeps.
- An alarm clock
- A thermos of ice water, with glasses, on a tray
- Bowl of fruit with tempting cookies, like

Walkers shortbread or the Prince of Wales's Duchy Originals biscuits
- Jar of Jelly Belly beans in exotic flavors like tangerine and kiwi, for those with a sweet tooth
- Notepad and pens for middle-of-the-night thoughts
- Small TV

On the Desk

- Postcards, stationery, and a cup of pens
- Disposable cameras

In the Bath

- Thick, absorbent terry cloth towels. I like the White House and Charisma brands.
- Special bath oils and soaps, in both masculine and feminine scents. I love almost any bath gel by Jo Malone or Molton Brown.
- Shampoo
- Extra toothpaste and toothbrushes. I'll keep a drawer stocked with all the things guests may have forgotten, like sunblock, aspirin, cold tablets, hairbrushes.
- Hair dryer
- New bars of soap. Buy little ones so you can offer a fresh bar of soap to each guest.
- Razors and shaving cream
- Terry cloth robes, in a size large enough to fit everyone, hanging on the back of the door

In the Closet

- Matching padded hangers
- Scented paper on shelves
- If you use this closet for out-of-season clothes, put them in long garment bags to get them out of your guest's way and keep the closet neater.

REFLECTIONS

Like all love affairs, this one, too, has reached another level. The frenzy has been replaced with an amazing peace. The remodeling is done, the walls are painted, the rooms are filled with furniture and art, and the shelves are bursting with books I hope to have time to read. The landscape has been tamed, and along the way I have had a chance to reflect on how very fortunate I have been.

As I walk into the house with John on a Friday evening, I have thought of those who have no homes. As I have gradually grown into a gardener, I have become more aware of the beauty of our environment and the urgent need to preserve it. My wonderful dogs have made me want to protect all abandoned animals. Now, when I sit on the porch, my thoughts no longer focus only on my own little corner but run more to what I can do with my time and resources to contribute to the world.

Someone else will eventually live at Manor House. The gardens may disappear again, the rooms will be painted other colors, but the happiness we have known here has been profound, and it has made me look outward. It has been very rewarding to host dinners to support local charities, to open the garden to the public for fundraisers. And so I suggest, if you have not already done so, to get involved in a cause you care about. It will make you feel more fulfilled as a person, and—who knows?—perhaps we can all work together to make a better world.

RIGHT: *This was a little shed attached to the kitchen and Alan decided to open it up and make a screened porch, retaining the original framing. John was thrilled to give his old wicker furniture a new coat of dark green paint and put it to use again. We found the rug in a Moroccan souk. Many a guest has sat on this porch with a cup of coffee, listening for the honking horn of our car—the signal that it's time to go off antiquing.*

RESOURCES

<table>
</table>

ANTIQUES

Shopping in America

There are so many good antiques dealers across the country that I could not begin to mention them all. If you are new to collecting, I suggest that you start by going to an antiques show in the city nearest you. Here you will meet many dealers and see what each has to offer. It's also helpful to subscribe to an antiques newspaper such as the *Newtown Bee* (www.newtownbee.com) to learn about upcoming auctions and shows.

CALIFORNIA

Foster-Gwin, Inc.
38 Hotaling Place
San Francisco, CA 94111
(415) 397-4986
fax: (415) 397-4988
www.fostergwin.com

Hollyhock
817 Hilldale Avenue
West Hollywood, CA 90069
(310) 777-0100
www.hollyhockinc.com

Mecox Gardens
919 North La Cienega Boulevard
Los Angeles, CA 90069
(310) 358-9272
www.mecoxgardens.com

Therien & Co.
716 North La Cienega Boulevard
Los Angeles, CA 90069
(310) 657-4615
www.therien.com

FLORIDA

Kevin L. Perry
127 South Pineapple Avenue
Sarasota, FL 34236
(813) 366-8483

Lars Bolander Limited
375 South County Road, Suite 105
Palm Beach, FL 33480
(561) 832-2121
www.larsbolander.com

Mecox Gardens
333 Worth Avenue
Palm Beach, FL 33405
(516) 805-8611
www.mecoxgardens.com

N. P. Trent Antiques
3729 South Dixie Highway
West Palm Beach, FL 33405
(561) 832-0919
www.nptrentantiques.com

Wilson Antiques
3716 South Dixie Highway
West Palm Beach, FL 33405
(561) 802-3881

GEORGIA

Jacqueline Adams Antiques and Interiors
2300 Peachtree Road NW, Suite B110
Atlanta, GA 30309
(404) 355-8123
www.jacquelineadamsantiques.com

Jane J. Marsden Antiques and Interiors
2300 Peachtree Road NW, Suite A102
Atlanta, GA 30309
(404) 355-1288
www.marsdenantiques.com

Jeff Littrell Antiques
178 Peachtree Hills Avenue
Atlanta, GA 30305
(404) 231-8662

Linda Horsley Antiques Inc.
425 Peachtree Hills Avenue NE, Suite 11A
Atlanta, GA 30305
(404) 467-0001

ILLINOIS

Alan Robandt & Co.
220 West Kinzie Street, 4th floor

Chicago, IL 60610
(312) 645-9995

Richard Norton Gallery
612 Merchandise Mart
Chicago, IL 60654
(312) 644-8855
www.richardnortongallery.com

NEW YORK
John Rosselli International
523 East 73rd Street
New York, NY 10021
(212) 772-2137
www.johnrosselliantiques.com

Lars Bolander
Red Horse Plaza
74 Montauk Highway, Unit 13
East Hampton, NY 11937
(631) 329-3400
www.larsbolander.com
or
72 Gansevoort Street
New York, NY 10014
(212) 924-1000

Mecox Gardens
66 Newtown Lane

East Hampton, NY 11937
(631) 329-9405
www.mecoxgardens.com
or
962 Lexington Avenue
New York, NY 10021
(212) 249-5301
or
257 Country Road 39A
Southampton, NY 11968
(631) 287-5015

NORTH CAROLINA
Randall Tysinger Antiques
208 North Elm Street
High Point, NC 27262
(877) 524-0080
www.randalltysinger.com

TENNESSEE
Marymont Plantation Shop
Westgate Center
6035 Highway 100
Nashville, TN 37205
(615) 352-4902

VIRGINIA
Kenny Ball Antiques and Accessories
2125 Ivy Road, Suite 7
Charlottesville, VA 22903
(434) 293-1361
www.kennyballantiques.com

WASHINGTON
Amano
1677 Wisconsin Avenue NW
Washington, D.C. 20007
(202) 298-7200
www.amano.bz

Marston Luce Antiques
1651 Wisconsin Avenue NW
Washington, D.C. 20007
(202) 333-6800

Susquehanna Antique Company, Inc.
3216 O Street NW
Washington, D.C. 20007
(202) 333-1511
www.susquehannaantiques.com

Shopping in Europe

If you would like to go shopping abroad, you might consider hiring a professional to help you plan your first trip. They will introduce you to the most interesting dealers and can also arrange to have your purchases shipped home.

ENGLAND
Alexander Cohane
8A Chelsea Studios
412 Fulham Road
London SW6, 1EB England
011.44.207.386.7674

FRANCE
PARIS
Floris Houwink
011.33.680.608.574

SOUTH OF FRANCE
Abilis—Michel Barma
9 Avenue Frederic Mistral
St. Remy-de-Provence, France 13210
011.33.4.90.92.57.34

ITALY
Oliva Busignani
Via San Domenico
21-50133
Florence, Italy
tel/fax: 011.39.055.575.034

Shipping

These reliable shippers will make sure your purchases arrive home safely. Contact them before your trip, and they will supply order booklets to take with you. At the end of the trip, you can wire money to them and they will pay the dealer, but you must make contact with them before you leave the United States.

LONDON AND PARIS
AirSea Packing
40-35 22nd Street
Long Island City, NY 11101
(718) 937-6800
www.airseapacking.com

AirSea Packing - London
AirSea House, Third Cross Road
Twickenham, TW2 5EB England
011.44.20.8893.3303
fax: 011.44.20.8893.3068

AirSea Packing - Paris
14, rue de la Pointe
93130 Noisy le Sec, France
011.33.1.48.46.81.42
fax: 011.33.1.48.46.03.33

Gander & White
21-44 44th Road
Long Island City, NY 11101
(718) 729-8877

SOUTH OF FRANCE
Abilis—Michel Barma
9 Avenue Frederic Mistral
St. Remy-de-Provence, France 13210
011.33.4.90.92.57.34

CHINA & GLASSWARE

Bardith Limited
901 Madison Avenue
New York, NY 10021
(212) 737-3775
or
31 East 72nd Street
New York, NY 10021
(212) 737-8660

Bergdorf Goodman
754 Fifth Avenue
New York, NY 10019
(212) 753-7300

China and Crystal by
William Yeoward at
Hollyhock
817 Hilldale Avenue
West Hollywood, CA 90069
(310) 777-0100
www.hollyhockinc.com

Country Dining Room Antiques
178 Main Street
Great Barrington, MA 01230
(413) 528-5050
www.countrydiningroomantiq.com

Crate & Barrel Nationwide
www.crateandbarrel.com

Elise Abrams Antiques
11 Stockbridge Road, Route 7
Great Barrington, MA 01230
(413) 528-3201
www.eliseabrams.com

Jane J. Marsden Antiques and Interiors
2300 Peachtree Road NW, Suite A102
Atlanta, GA 30309
(404) 355-1288
www.marsdenantiques.com

Pearl River Mart
477 Broadway
New York, NY 10013
(212) 431-4770
(800) 878-2446
www.pearlriver.com

Scully & Scully
504 Park Avenue
New York, NY 10022
(212) 755-2590

TABLE LINENS & FABRICS

Retail Stores

ABC Carpet & Home
888 Broadway
New York, NY 10003
(212) 473-3000
www.abchome.com

Anthropologie
(800) 309-2500
www.anthropologie.com

Pier 1 Imports
(800) 245-4595
www.pier1.com

Custom Linens

Anichini Inc.
230 Fifth Avenue, Suite 1990
New York, NY 10001
(212) 679-9540
www.anichini.com

Casa del Bianco
866 Lexington Avenue
New York, NY 10021
(212) 249-9224
www.casadelbianco.com

Julia Boutique
70 Arch Street
Greenwich, CT 07830
(203) 422-2216
www.juliaboutique.com

Leron
804 Madison Avenue
New York, NY 10021
(212) 753-6700
www.leron.com

ART

If you want to start collecting art in a serious way, I suggest that you contact an art consultant who can advise you on both dealers and auctions.

Kim M. Heirston Art Advisory
10 East 63rd Street
New York, NY 10021
(212) 588-1234

Mallory Hathaway
Mallory Hathaway Fine Arts
150 East 61st Street
New York, NY 10021
(212) 308-0009
mhathaway@ncy.rr.com

DESIGN & GARDENING BOOKS

Corner Bookstore
1313 Madison Avenue
New York, NY 10128
(212) 831-3554
fax: (212) 831-2930

Hayden & Fandetta
310 West 55th Street, Apt. 5H
New York, NY 10019
or
P.O. Box 1549 Radio City Station
New York, NY 10101-1549
(212) 582-2505

Johnnycake Books
12 Academy Street
Salisbury, CT 06068

(860) 435-6677
fax: 860-435-6688
www.johnnycakebooks.com

Lenox Hill Bookstore
1018 Lexington Avenue
New York, NY 10021
(212) 472-7170
fax: (212) 772-1790

Potterton Books, Ltd.
Decoration and Design Building
979 Third Avenue, #101
New York, NY 10022
(212) 644-2292

Out-of-print/Second-hand Books

Glen Horowitz Bookseller
87 Newtown Lane
East Hampton, NY 11937
(631) 324-5511
or
152 East 74th Street
New York, NY 10021
(212) 327-3538

Jane Stubbs Books at
Bergdorf Goodman
754 Fifth Avenue, 7th floor
New York, NY 10019
(212) 753-7300

Strand Bookstore
828 Broadway
New York, NY 10003
(212) 473-1452
fax: (212) 473-2591

Online:

www.alibris.com
www.barnesandnoble.com

GARDENS

Garden Furniture and Ornaments

There are so many wonderful places where you can find special containers and ornaments (both antique and new) for the outdoors. I recommend attending one of the following garden shows, where you can count on seeing amazing items. Many dealers do not have shops, so this is a great way to make contacts.

Garden Furniture Shows

Chicago Botanical Garden Antiques and
Garden Show
1000 Lake Cook Road
Glencoe, IL 60022
www.chicagobotanic.org

The Nashville Antiques and Garden Show
601 Commerce Street
Nashville, TN 37203
www.antiquesandgardenshow.com

NY Botanical Garden Antiques
and Garden Show
200th Street and Kazimiroff Boulevard
Bronx, NY 10458
(718) 817-8700
www.nybg.org

Antique Garden Furniture Dealers

Barbara Israel
296 Mount Holly Road
Katonah, NY 10536
(914) 232-4271

Fleur, Inc.
84 Lexington Avenue
Mount Kisco, NY 10549
(914) 241-3400

Michael D. Trapp Inc.
7 River Road, Box 67
West Cornwall, CT 06796
(860) 672-6098

Treillage
418 East 75th Street
New York, NY 10021
(212) 535-2288
fax: (212) 517-6589
www.treillageonline.com

Plants

Bluebird Nursery, Inc. (wholesale)
519 Bryan Street
Clarkson, NE
(800) 356-9164
fax: (402) 892-3738
www.bluebirdnursery.com

Forest Farm
990 Tetherow Road
Williams, OR 97544-9599
(541) 846-7269
fax: (541) 846-6963
www.forestfarm.com

Glass House Works
Church Street
P.O. Box 97
Stewart, OH 45778-0097
(740) 662-2142
fax: (740) 662-2120
www.glasshouseworks.com

Heronswood Nursery Ltd
7530 NE 288th Street
Kingston, WA 98346
(360) 297-4172
www.heronswood.com

Plant Delights Nursery, Inc.
9241 Sauls Road
Raleigh, NC 27603
(919) 772-4794
fax: (919) 662-0370
www.plantdelights.com

You can also google (www.google.com) whatever plant you are looking for and contact the specialty nurseries that appear on the list.

Bulbs

Brent & Becky's Bulbs
7900 Daffodil Lane
Gloucester, VA 23061

(804) 693-3966
fax: (804) 693-9436
www.brentandbeckysbulbs.com

Connell's Dahlias
10616 Waller Road East
Tacoma, WA 98446
(253) 531-0292
fax: (253) 536-7725
www.connells-dahlias.com

K. van Bourgondien & Sons, Inc.
P.O. Box 2000
Virginia Beach, VA 23450
(800) 622-9997
www.dutchbulbs.com

Swan Island Dahlias
P.O. Box 700
Canby, OR 97013
(503) 266-7711
www.dahlias.com

Van Engelen Inc.
23 Tulip Drive
P.O. Box 638
Bantam, CT 06750
(800) 567-8734
www.vanengelen.com

Seeds

Baker Creek Heirloom Seeds
2278 Baker Creek Road
Mansfield, MO 65704
(417) 924-8917
fax: (417) 924-8887
www.rareseeds.com

Chiltern Seeds
Boutree Stile
Ulverston, Cumbria
LA12, 7PB England
011.44.122.958.1137

fax: 011.44.122.958.4549
www.chilternseeds.co.uk

Johnny's Selected Seeds
184 Foss Hill Road
Albion, Maine 04910-9731
(207) 861-3900
www.johnnyseeds.com

Seed Savers Exchange
3076 North Winn Road
Decorah, IA 52101
(563) 382-5990
fax: (563) 382-5872
www.seedsavers.org

Seeds of Change
P.O. Box 15700
Santa Fe, NM 87592-1500
(888) 762-7333
www.seedsofchange.com

Select Seeds
180 Stickney Hill Road
Union, CT 06076-4617
(860) 684-0395
www.selectseeds.com

Thompson & Morgan
P.O. Box 1308
Jackson, NJ 08527-0308
(800) 274-7333
fax: (888) 466-4769
www.thompson-morgan.com

Selected Gardens to Visit

Huntington Botanical Gardens
1151 Oxford Road
San Marino, CA 91108
(818) 405-2100

Longwood Gardens
Route 1, P.O. Box 501
Kennett Square, PA 19348
(610) 388-1000
(800) 737-5500 (toll-free)

Old Westbury Gardens
75 Old Westbury Road
Old Westbury, NY 11568
(516) 333-0048

Wave Hill
West 249th Street and
Independence Avenue
(right on Henry Hudson Parkway)
Bronx, NY 10471

RECIPE INDEX

GUEST BARN